In DURGA'S EMBRACE

In DURGA'S EMBRACE

A DISCIPLE'S DIARY

SWAMI DURGANANDA

TIMELESS BOOKS
2006

timeless books
www.timeless.org

© 2006 timeless books

In Canada:
Box 9, Kootenay Bay, BC   V0B 1X0
contact@timeless.org
(800) 661-8711

In the United States:
P.O. Box 3543, Spokane, WA   99220-3543
info@timeless.org
(800) 251-9273

Cover photograph by Andrea Rollefson
Design by Todd Stewart   www.breeree.com

Printed in Canada on 100% post-consumer-waste recycled acid-free paper.

ISBN-10: 1-932018-12-3
ISBN-13: 978-1-932018-12-7

Library and Archives Canada Cataloguing in Publication

Durgananda, Swami, 1924–
    In Durga's embrace : a disciple's diary / Swami Durgananda.

ISBN 1-932018-12-3

    1. Durgananda, Swami, 1924–. 2. Spiritual biography—United States.
I. Title.

BL1175.D858A3 2006   294.5'092   C2005-907101-X

This book is dedicated to my Guru, Swami Sivananda Radha, who taught me the importance of awareness in even the smallest details. She inspired me to bring gratitude into this final stage of my life, each day a gift lived with joy and a desire to serve. She also helped me to discover my Durga nature, which brought me the balance I needed in my inner being and a connection to Divine Mother or Krishna or Jesus or Buddha – it really doesn't matter, as they are all One.

table of contents

foreword

One image stands out in my mind when I think about Swami Durgananda and her Guru, Swami Radha: Durgananda is in her seventies and Swami Radha is in her eighties. Durgananda bends down to help Swami Radha out of her chair. They stand together for a moment, in each other's arms. Swami Radha kisses Durgananda gently on the cheek. The two look steadily at each other. They are very good friends; they are disciple and guru.

I have known Swami Durgananda, then Margaret White, since 1978. We met at Yasodhara Ashram, both of us mothers and householders, making the transition from family life to serious spiritual life. She became a swami in 1989. I remember being so impressed that Margaret, at sixty-five, would take the radical step of renunciation. Here was an older woman, still willing to make changes in her life, and ready to take on such a powerful initiation. The name Durga seemed perfect for her path. It was important for me to see her fulfilling her dedication, choosing her name and putting her ideals into practice. It let me know that I could do it, too.

In 1994 Swami Durgananda initiated me into *sanyas,* acting for Swami Radha. I, too, entered into this lineage of women teachers, a very rare and exciting thing. Having a woman teacher of yoga, a *yogini,* emphasizes the feminine principle of Divine life. Swami Radha referred to her Guru, Swami Sivananda, as her spiritual mother; Swami Radha's disciples called her Mataji (mother). Like a mother, Swami Radha was always concerned about her students. There was a deep caring – she was full of love and encouragement. There was time for personal talks and advice for personal growth. It was all practical and related to the events in our daily lives – everything was ultimately spiritual.

Swami Radha encouraged us as women to find our own unique way as her disciples, and to access the feminine qualities such as strength, endurance and the ability to really care. It has been an amazing process to see how the qualities of the goddess Durga were engaged in the transformation of Margaret White. Durga is fierce, she fights the demons of doubt, and she cuts away attachments. It is the fierceness of the Light and the desire for transformation that shines through Swami Durgananda.

If anyone thinks it is easy to let go of old habits and ways of thinking and create a whole new way of being, you have only to remember how hard it is to let go of something you are attached to on the physical level. Then move this process to letting go of thoughts and concepts of who you are, which are harder to recognize and much more complex. This is the challenge of renunciation – to realize that who you are is not an intellectual exercise, but a lived experience.

Now in her eighties, Swami Durgananda is an inspiring teacher, bringing the wisdom of her experience into the teaching of Dream, Kundalini and Hatha Yoga. It is so wonderful to see her teaching Hatha Yoga to elders and youth, leading Kundalini and Dream classes and being an integral part of the Ashram. She embodies the teachings, and her dedication shines through.

When you read her story, you will see how the teachings of yoga can really be translated into daily life. The awareness is developed day by day, by reflecting on ordinary events. The thread of Swami Durgananda's devotion and commitment to her Guru kept guiding her through her later years. Swami Radha obviously valued having a student so close to her own age that she could trust and talk to. One that was willing to keep learning.

Swami Durgananda's diary is a record of her relationship with Swami Radha. In it, she reveals the tender moments and the challenging moments that are part of the guru-disciple relationship. Her story is also about being a student no matter how old you are and about loyalty to and love for her teacher. It's about having and being a true friend. Walking together.

– Swami Radhananda, Yasodhara Ashram, January 2006

a word from the author

When I met Swami Radha in 1967, I didn't know what a guru was or what the responsibilities were of becoming a disciple. I didn't know that the guru dispels the darkness of ignorance in the disciple's mind. I am sure each guru has a different way of doing this. In fact, I observed Swami Radha using different ways with those around her. At times she would even tell one student to do the opposite of what she had just told another student to do. There is a danger in assuming one student's experience of the guru's personal teaching is the only way. My diaries show only what I experienced and what I needed to learn for my own evolution. So, if this book can be of help to others, that is fine, but it is wise to remember that others may have had different kinds of experiences and learning from her.

A guru often teaches lessons in what seems like a totally irrational or unfair way. But a guru's teaching on the spiritual path has a very different purpose from teaching in the ordinary way. What appears to be extreme behaviour or unusually harsh words is to be taken in for reflection and learning. However, a true guru will never intentionally do anything or ask the disciple to do anything that goes against the disciple's conscience. This is where the disciple must take responsibility to question and clarify and even refrain from doing something recommended by the guru if it goes against his or her conscience. This takes careful discrimination, because it is very easy for ego and self-will to step in.

In my difficult interactions with Swami Radha, I never felt that she was demanding something that would hurt me beyond causing pain to my ego. And I knew that the areas she was highlighting for me were those I had to work on. But she had also given me the gift of a mantra and prepared me for *sanyas* initiation[1] that linked us together and made my commitment clear. That is why I kept going through the hard times. I wanted to do my best to achieve the potential she was pointing out to me, to find out for myself if what she said was true. And this was what she encouraged us all to do, to question, reflect, put into practice and discover for ourselves.

Swami Radha as a guru was very down to earth and practical. She gave inspiring talks to me personally, to small and large groups, using personal examples to bring the teachings alive. But she didn't leave it at that. She told us to put these teachings into practice and write about what we learned. If all we did was repeat back to her what she had said, we were just using her talks as entertainment.

She often reminded us to review our diaries, dreams and reflections. In the process of writing this book I have discovered the tremendous source of learning in the material I have recorded over the years, as I had never gone through the entire collection at one time. Lessons that I needed to take into my core I saw repeated. Problems in my relationships were not solved in one encounter but needed continuing attention. Issues that Swami Radha highlighted took various forms that she constantly brought to my awareness. The practices she gave me opened a deeper layer in my being. And seeing the detailed unfolding of my life over the years with her I have become aware of the block-by-block construction of my "cathedral of consciousness." It took patience on Swami Radha's part as well as my own. But the rewards in my understanding have been worth it all.

You will find long lapses between diary entries in the first chapter

---

1   *Sanyas* is the initiation and vows to become a swami.

of this book, which covers the period from 1967–1978. I wanted to give the highlights of how Swami Radha came into my life. At that time, the power of what I had already set in motion caught me in a web of activities and responsibilities. It took me eleven years to finally free myself to come to her Ashram, where the second part of my life journey began. The real story is during this time, as a student of Swami Radha. My connection with Swami Radha blossomed as I lived and worked with her in her community in British Columbia and Spokane, Washington.

I have included dreams that are an important thread through my story and they are in italics to separate them from any commentary I made. I have also changed some of the names of the resident members of the Ashram, to be sensitive to those who have either since left the Ashram or whom I could not reach to tell them about my journals being published.

I would like to thank the members of the Yasodhara Ashram editorial board, Swami Radhananda, Swami Gopalananda, Swami Lalitananda and Clea McDougall, for their support and encouragement to keep expanding my thoughts about this story.

I also want to thank Karin Lenman, Roseanne Harvey and Kendra Ward, who all worked closely with me in editing the book. Thank you to timeless books' publisher, Andrew Wedman. And thanks to all the people who read my manuscript and gave me their suggestions along the way.

Finally, I would like to thank the Ashram residents for supporting my process over the years, and my family for their understanding and caring.

introduction

My story is about how I came to live with my Guru, how she taught me through her example and through our day-to-day interactions. I developed a caring relationship with her that grew deeper over the years I lived with her. She set me on a path toward higher consciousness, what she called the path of Liberation. For me, this meant liberation from my own weaknesses, the issues that kept me bound to my little self, the personality aspects that interfered with my connection to my higher self. I was a late bloomer and a slow learner, but I stayed with it.

What was it that drew me, an ordinary housewife living in the suburbs of Philadelphia, to become a swami of an ashram in British Columbia? Part of my story is discovering now that there were signs all along the way that pointed to my future direction. But it was like a jigsaw puzzle with pieces that had to be found and fit in the proper place.

I only found those pieces in hindsight, as I had not recognized each message as anything significant at the time. And as I discovered one piece after another, what came to light was that I had a very patient knowing aspect of myself that was gently guiding me in a particular direction every step of the way. When the overall picture of my life became clear, I realized that I had indeed followed my life's purpose and that has been a very affirming insight for me as I move into the latter years of my life.

At the Quaker school I attended for thirteen years, from kindergarten through the twelfth grade, I began to understand the idea of inner Light, as we sat quietly once a week in the Meeting House. No images, no dogma, no ritual – just sitting quietly and listening within. As a small child, I had squirmed and longed for the meeting to end. But in this Quaker school environment I learned about ethics, quality, creativity – I was challenged to use my mind.

The school seal expressed for me what my life was to be about. It showed the vibrant figure of an angel stepping through a wide-open door with the sea behind him. On it, the words from the Book of Revelation offer a promise of vast potential: "Behold, I have set before thee an open door." In this seal, I see choice, courage, freedom, a willingness to serve.

During World War II, I attended Wellesley College, but left to get married, and my direction was set. That deeper knowing part of myself was buried in a life filled with raising three children, doing volunteer work, furthering my education, teaching, and the many, many things that make up a woman's life. I struggled, wanting to do my best, drawing on values and examples from my past. I learned patience and persistence. And I learned to extend myself, to put others first. My life was full and productive, but I felt there was something missing and began the search for more meaning. The children were growing up and my son moved out on his own in 1966, the summer that my father died.

I was close to my father and one afternoon shortly after his death, I was lying on my bed feeling particularly sad and alone. I cried out to a power greater than myself, "There must be some direction for me to follow. How can I find it? Bring me into contact with people of like mind, who are also seeking the Divine. I want to bring more meaning into my life. Please show me the way."

Within a few months, I received a letter inviting me to join an Edgar Cayce[1] group called A Search for God. I had no idea how they

---

1   Edgar Cayce was a well-known clairvoyant who died in the 1950s. Swami Radha had a close connection with his son, Hugh Lynn Cayce, and his organization, The Association for Research and Enlightenment.

got my name but it was just what I was looking for. I joined the group, met other people who were searching, and started some meditation and reflective practices growing out of our meetings each week. It was when some of us went to the Cayce Headquarters in Virginia Beach for a workshop in the spring of 1967 that I met Swami Sivananda Radha.

one | MEETING MY GURU

April 16, 1967, Virginia

I come out of the main building of the Edgar Cayce Headquarters after breakfast to take a walk before our morning session begins. My eyes are drawn to a figure across from me, a woman striding confidently and with purpose, her orange sari contrasting with the white building. I watch her and think what a powerful yet unassuming woman she is. There is a radiance about her. She does not seem short in stature yet I realize that she is not actually as tall as she appears. There is something about her that attracts me, something that is elusive, something I cannot pin down. I watch her until she turns the corner and disappears from my view. She is Swami Sivananda Radha, the speaker whom I have come all the way from Philadelphia to hear in this two-day workshop on the Book of Revelation East and West.

In the workshop, Swami Radha says, "Be very careful what kind of desires you have. The only really important desire to ask for – to always have for future lives – is love for God, Cosmic Love. Give back to God all other foolish loves that are only in your way." This makes me really think about my life and where I am right now. Love for God is my heart's desire. But what are all the foolish loves she mentions?

She shows slides of the symbols for the chakras of the Eastern Kundalini system and makes a connection between this system and Cayce's approach through the symbolism of the Book of Revelation. It is more than I can absorb all at once, but I have made notes with little sketches of the slides so I can bring back some of the ideas she has expressed.

She is down to earth, practical yet inspiring.

April 17, 1967

Today, Swami Radha teaches us an ancient spiritual practice called the Divine Light Invocation[1] that she learned in India.

We form a circle and she instructs us to fill ourselves with Light and to see and feel the Light as we allow it to flow out of our heart centres and our hands. She repeats the mantra of the Light Invocation:

I am created by Divine Light
I am sustained by Divine Light
I am protected by Divine Light
I am surrounded by Divine Light
I am ever growing into Divine Light

I feel an impact in my entire body as I follow her instructions. We visualize the planet Earth out in space and wrap the Light around it to protect it. I have a strange feeling of being grounded firmly here on the Earth, yet at the same time seeing the mysterious form of the planet Earth floating out in space shimmering in the Light. It is like being in two worlds at the same time, connected by Light.

I am deeply touched by Swami Radha. There is so much to digest from this workshop, and I want to learn more.

---

1   See Swami Sivananda Radha, *The Divine Light Invocation* (Kootenay Bay, BC: timeless books, 2001/2006).

April 29, 1967 Philadelphia

I have discovered that Swami Radha will be giving a talk in Philadelphia on Mantra Yoga. I can hardly believe my good fortune to hear her again. She will be speaking in an old farmhouse near here that has been turned into a centre with rooms for classes and lectures.

April 30, 1967

I arrive early but already the room is full and people are sitting in the small adjoining hallway. I sit on the stairs where I can partially see into the room and am able to hear everything. When Swami Radha starts to chant the mantra *Hari Om*, I feel myself lifted up on the pure sound of her voice. I close my eyes and am enveloped in those clear notes. *Hari Om* reaches a deep place inside me.

September 21, 1967

Outside gardening today, I catch myself singing an irritating toothpaste jingle over and over. How inane can I be? Why do I sing those annoying commercials? What is my mind doing? Then I remember Swami Radha's advice about repeating an affirmation or a mantra over and over. I switch to the *Hari Om* mantra. Like a miracle, the mantra replaces the jingle and all the other mental background noise.

May 1, 1968

Our Cayce study group invited Swami Radha to meet with us as part of her spring tour. I am so happy to see her again. In my morning meditation I thought about questions I have for Swami Radha. What came was a kind of waking dream of me under the ocean poking in the sand with a long fork. Oil gushes up out of the water. I wonder what it means. Oil is a valuable source of energy, so it must have something to say about tapping into a vast source of energy in the depths of my unconscious.

When Swami Radha meets with our group, what stands out for me are her instructions for the Divine Light Invocation. The man who stands beside her when we do the Light Invocation tells me afterward that he was nearly bowled over by the impact of the energy he felt. I am glad to learn this practice again because now I feel more confident about doing it. My niece, Dawn, also came to the meeting. She is a member of the group and I am so glad that someone in my family is interested.

May 3, 1968

I feel drawn to Swami Radha and have gone to hear her speak at two other locations. I want to hear her as much as possible while she is in the area. However, it is strange that in spite of being uplifted by my contacts with her, I am feeling upset physically and in turmoil spiritually. I am inspired but at the same time feel inadequate, as if something is missing in me. She is shaking up some of my concepts about who I am or who I think I am.

I had a dream that tells me of my inner garbage:

I am in Paris. Water is running down the middle of the streets. I have some garbage and sewage in a bag that I have to get rid of. I dump the bag into the flowing water as this is what everyone does. I feel rather strange doing this.

How will I actually do this in my life?

July 3, 1968

I received a letter from Swami Radha today about the dream I sent to her in May. She writes, "Your dream is indeed interesting. Running water is a very good symbol. The garbage that you dumped into the water may be all your worries, and if you dump all your worries into the running water of the Spirit, then you have something to look forward to indeed.... I am sure we will meet again. We do not know when but I shall be happy to hear from you. Give my love and blessings to the group members and accept my wish for you to be ever in the Divine Light."

With all that's going on in my life, I really wonder how we are going to meet again. I have just been accepted for a teaching position I applied for. It will be a major focus and my first real job teaching art. But I also have family responsibilities and the Cayce group, as well as my volunteer work at Planned Parenthood where I counsel young women. Also this branch of Planned Parenthood has offered me the opportunity to do some artwork for a mental health project. I am taking on a lot.

But I don't want to start worrying as Swami Radha says that in my dream I have dumped my worries in the water.

May 12, 1972

I am becoming more and more intrigued with my dreams and the messages they give me. I write them down but I know there is more to be discovered. It is always easier to see the guidance they have when I look back from a different perspective. Reviewing them regularly helps to clarify the symbols and the messages that are repeated as my inner Self tries to make me aware of what needs to be done. When I add daily comments on my life to accompany my dreams, then I can see the connection between the dream and circumstances in my life. This growing relationship is like finding a new friend.

May 21, 1972

I am talking on the phone to Swami Radha. Some of her colleagues are complaining because I have tied up the phone so long trying to get through. She is very lovely and calm. I tell her about a dream I had in which I was doing a finger painting in vivid colours. I want her advice. I can't remember what she said.

It is interesting that I contact her in my dream to tell her about a dream. I must be really trying to connect with her. I want to convey something to her and want her advice, but I am unable to recall what she said. I am missing out on something. Of course, on another level, this is about contacting my higher self. I now have someone who symbolizes this aspect of myself.

I want to keep in touch with her, and send her donations and my homemade Christmas cards each year.

September 28, 1973

I have been having a lot of dreams of hiding, imprisonment and escape. Last night I dreamt:

Watching a film of a young man, a prisoner on an island, undergoing torture. As he is sentenced, he yells out passionately, "I won't fall asleep! I won't sleep like everyone else!" And it is no longer a film. I join him as we make an escape because the guards are asleep.

I am developing awareness of how I keep myself in a prison of narrow concepts. I feel insecure, doubt myself and set unrealistic standards of perfection. I seek solutions outside myself instead of addressing the longing I feel inside, and I allow my pride to prevent me from openly dealing with the conflicts in my marriage.

Often in arguments with my husband our minds seem to be on parallel lines miles apart with no chance of coming together in understanding. The emotions are intense and I feel there can be no resolution. I turn away, go into the bedroom and shut the door. I am in tears, knowing that this is not solving the issue, but pride and stubborn resistance hold me bound.

May 1, 1975

I am visiting a school where my daughter, Wendy, as a small child, is attending second grade. There are two teachers, a man and a woman. They give out awards of money to students for their good work in arithmetic. Next they point out the children who have lost money by doing the work incorrectly. The first little boy has lost 40 cents. Wendy is next and looks miserable. I rush up and tell the teachers I think it is a disgrace that they do this to the children. It is humiliating and ruins the whole purpose of school. Learning is supposed to be fun and exciting.

In the dream I feel uplifted and righteous as I defend Wendy;

then negative from the powerful emotions, expressing my anger. The teachers are having the children make some kind of accounting but using money puts it in the wrong light.

When I look at the emotions of anger and humiliation in this dream and I begin to settle down, to become quiet, to listen within, the thought comes to me: "Be still and know that I am God." Then an inner voice speaks:

"You must learn to accept the parts that make you who you are. You are part of peace and joy, but you block it by setting up inner barriers. You expect and demand too much. Relax and let that oneness flow through and around you. Feel the power and warmth of the setting sun and know that power is in you as well. Just BE and know the beauty it can bring. Remember that even the least part of yourself has its place. Accept all and love all."

I am moved by these words that have such a deep understanding and I look at the dream in a different light. A school is a place to learn. Two teachers who represent a balance of masculine and feminine in myself are teaching me a lesson. They are working with an immature part of me. They are using one of the standards I have chosen in my outer life, money. Even though I have rejected the concept of money as being important, its influence still forces its way into my mind. I am being shown that one must pay the price for going about a lesson in the wrong way. I act like a child thinking it is unfair and I rebel. But it has nothing to do with children or school or money in a literal external way.

Learning the lesson; paying the price; youth learns from wisdom. I am in the school of life to learn and I must be open to the guidance of my inner teachers. I may not like their methods but they are telling me that right action will be rewarded while improper action must be paid for. I don't like to hear this and protect the vulnerable immature part of me. There is a price for many learning experiences. I choose my own price whether I know it or not. I may want to avoid a difficult lesson or not face the facts. Learning is often painful, but to grow I must go through suffering and give up control. This is a humbling process for the ego and a necessary one for spiritual growth. It is easier to rebel than to face embarrassment or to admit that I have done something less than perfectly.

I see how deeply ingrained is my need for perfection. I am striving too hard and the result is perfectionism, which is self-defeating. What is "perfect," anyway? Just accepting myself and doing the best I know in the moment without driving myself. Also I think if I am perfect I will be appreciated. But as I reflect on the message I realize that wanting to be appreciated means I am feeling insecure.

The dream also shows the importance of accounting for the things I do in my life. I do not pay for errors with money but through precious energy that is wasted in careless behaviour or negative emotions. Money represents resources, the most valuable of which is energy. Dreams can have several messages, which I may not get all at once, but they are all meaningful.

Looking at the need to be appreciated, I see that I am not appreciating myself. I feel a lack of appreciation in my marriage. As my husband and I drift further apart there is an underlying, unspoken tension that often erupts in sarcasm or cutting remarks. I feel insecure, hesitant to address the situation, and so I dream of hiding and escaping. But I am hiding not only from the truth of my marital situation, but also from the need to bring forth the Light within. I need to appreciate myself and know that the Divine always accepts me as I am. That is all that matters.

March 30, 1976

A letter from Swami Radha! Every time I receive a note from her I feel something calling me. There is a longing mixed with anxiety about what this means in my future. There is a sense of urgency. I need to take action but at the same time I am uncertain.

Swami Radha writes: "Thank you very much for your gift. It would be nice if we could meet each other again. What are your prospects of coming out West? Maybe a few of your circle could travel out here in the good season, do a little sightseeing on the way. In the warm weather you could tent, and you could share the gas and food. Allow yourself to dream a little, express your wishes and someday they will come about. I would like to send you a tape. Let me know which subjects you are interested in. Many blessings."

I feel I should not take anything from her, as she needs the money for so many things. But then I realize that is not being gracious so I write back asking for *The Power of Mantras,* as I want to know more about mantra.

I have been listening to other of Swami Radha's tapes and even going to sleep with the *Hari Om* mantra. Her tapes give me this feeling of urgency that I don't quite understand. Her talks touch me on a deep level, inspiring me, and at the same time they are so down to earth and practical. Her words from the *Liberation* tape keep coming back: "Weed your own garden." She says there is plenty to do there and you don't have to be concerned about weeding your neighbour's garden. I need to apply this to my family and refrain from expressing concern about how they live their lives.

May 13, 1976

I had a dream of majestic mountains in the distance. Swami Radha lives in the mountains, but I feel that I am far from being ready to ascend mountains. When I listen to *The Power of Mantras* tape she sent me, I feel as if she is speaking to me personally with powerful clarity and directness. She could be sitting across the table looking right at me, drawing me in. Why do I feel that sense of being drawn in and yet a bit scared? Drawn into what? What does it involve?

May 14, 1976

I dreamt about a feeling of impending change in my world that is of vital importance:

The feeling is associated with the arrival of a great spiritual leader who will emerge to guide us into a new age. There is a dangerous situation having to do with pollution but I am convinced that the spiritual leader will be able to solve this problem. I am very excited about it and tell other people. I have a feeling that I am going to join a crusade of some sort and will eventually join up with followers of the spiritual leader.

This dream refers to an important change in me. The spiritual leader is either my higher self emerging to lead me in the right direction, or it is Swami Radha, who has been on my mind so much. The pollution is negative thoughts, dangerous to my spiritual development. There is clarity and strength in this dream.

September 5, 1976

I have an appointment with Swami Radha at 8:45 p.m. When I meet with her she slaps me on the left side of my face. It stings and I start to cry softly. I don't understand why she did it.

When I wake up I realize the slap was more of a surprise than a hurt. I need that to wake me up. It is so easy to slip back, to go to sleep, to forget.

This dream is a reminder from my higher self to pay attention to what is going on in my life. I am blessed right now to have precious free time that I must not waste by getting involved in too many activities. I need to establish a pattern for spiritual growth, incorporating my dreams and the Divine Light Invocation that has given me a connection with Swami Radha.

Yet when I think about my marriage situation I am totally amazed at how I can swing back and forth so completely between two aspects of myself. At one extreme I want to break free, be totally independent, be just what I want to be, unencumbered by any surroundings that might distract me from working toward inner growth. This "I" says I must do something drastic to break the unending cycle that is repeating itself over and over, the same issues, the same struggles.

But the other "I" says, "No. You have to grow within the limitations that you have chosen. In fact, those very limitations are what you need to use to work on yourself. In this way you learn to transform, to love, to take the other person into account. To escape from it externally means that the same situations will continue to be attracted to you – until you learn to rise above them. Then it won't matter where you are because you will have conquered it." What to do? Both voices have a point. I have a long way to go. I still have a demanding ego.

June 13, 1977

I am back at my childhood house. I go down into the cellar carefully to check it out, moving slowly and looking around cautiously. I am amazed to see it has been cleaned out except for a shelf of jellies and preserves. The laundry room has been painted white and is bare.

This dream seems to be saying I have cleared out a lot of stuff in the cellar of my unconscious. So I am working on myself. But Swami Radha seems so far away and there are so many unknown factors.

Now another complication has arisen and my husband is ill. He has been in and out of the hospital. Visiting him there and taking care of him when he is home brings us closer together. We read books aloud and have time to talk about our situation. But this creates increasing confusion as I feel pulled more strongly in two directions.

March 12, 1978, Florida

A few weeks ago, after my husband's recovery we both felt we needed to get away and we took a trip to Florida to visit friends for a week. Our daughter Carla was looking after Jason, our golden retriever. Yesterday, Jason got out of the yard and was hit by a car. Carla was in tears on the phone when she told us what happened. I was in shock and barely heard her words, unable to take in that he was gone. Jason was my constant companion at home or in the car. Why has this happened? Is there a karmic reason? Over and over, I ask myself, why, why?

March 24, 1978, Philadelphia

Today, while driving alone, I think that I hear Jason panting in the back, although I know it's impossible. Tears begin to flow and I am overwhelmed by a sense of emptiness. Suddenly I hear a clear voice coming from inside:

"How dare you act like this? Would you grieve if you knew Jason had been taken for something better? How do you know the purpose and plan of things beyond your understanding?"

I feel stunned and humbled and ashamed. When I chant *Hari Om* a feeling of peace and acceptance envelops me. There is something greater at work here.

I finally accept that this is Divine intervention, part of making way for my next step. I see the bigger picture. My strong attachment to the dog was holding me back. He had become the companion I missed in my marriage. Swami Radha called these jarring events the two-by-four that comes when we have taken too long to respond to the signs we are given.

It is definitely time to go to the Ashram. I call my niece, Dawn, as she knows about the Ashram from Swami Radha's visit. I ask her if she is interested in going to the Ten Days of Yoga course in May and she responds with enthusiasm. "Yes, what a great idea. I will have to make arrangements but I am sure it will work out." How fortunate I am to have a family member who is interested in the spiritual path.

two | METAMORPHOSIS

June 2, 1978 Yasodhara Ashram

The Ashram is nestled in the mountains at the end of a cedar-lined road. When Dawn and I walk into the guest lodge, we immediately feel at home, connecting to the smell of the cedar walls that remind us of the family summer cottage in Connecticut. We find our room and I put down my duffel bag and sit on one of the beds, looking around. We didn't know what to expect. Would we be sleeping on a mattress on the floor? Would we be in a large dormitory with a dozen other people?

We never expected a beautiful room like this with furniture for two and a closet big enough for plenty of clothes plus storage. Through the large front window I see the lake sparkling through the trees, the mountains rising up behind. Through the side window my attention goes to a large rock on the edge of the forest. It looks like the head of a serpent, its mouth partially open. It could be putting out words of wisdom for those who can understand, or it might be warning evil forces to stay away. It is like a guardian of the guest lodge.

After settling in I take a walk up the road alone, needing to get some exercise and time to reflect. I take in the rich smell of the earth and the evergreen trees. So I am here at last. Why did it take me so long? I am so happy that I feel at home; it is familiar although I have never been in British Columbia before. There is a sense of magic, something waiting to be revealed. I feel the openness and freedom of the space, the fullness of the silence.

I know that I have come because of Swami Radha and her encouragement. But also something has been missing in my life. This is a key point, as I have decisions to make about my marriage. Should I stay in it and work on growing and learning through it, learning to be inwardly free no matter what the outer circumstances are? Or does the marriage and the environment it creates interfere with my spiritual development?

Our marriage has a bond of caring strengthened by years of good times and hard times, even suffering. Yet our driving goals and life aims are heading in totally different directions. I am drawn to an inner spiritual focus, self-awareness, reading, studying, attuning body, mind and spirit, putting my ideals into practice by volunteering for activities that have meaning for me. My husband is wrapped up in the outer world, his hobbies, his career, connections through his work. Would each of us be happier living alone?

I look around me as I walk and everything I see has special meaning. The boughs of the evergreen trees seem to bend down to bless me as I walk by. I look across the lake and see the powerful image of a huge sea creature that appears to be carved into the side of the mountain. How did it get there? It tells me that this whole area is sacred ground.

When I return from my walk Dawn and I go down to supper. As we walk into the main building I see Swami Radha standing in an adjoining room, talking to some people. She seems shorter than I remember from our meeting ten years ago. Have I carried a sense of her being larger than she is because of what she emanates? We approach her to introduce ourselves and she welcomes us warmly. "So at last you have come to the Ashram. You must have lunch with me tomorrow. We will eat outside in my screen house. Then we will have time to talk together." I thank her, and my heart pounds at just the thought of meeting with her.

June 3, 1978

Today when we have lunch, Swami Radha tells me I have come home! This really touches my heart, but I wonder, is she saying I am a part of the Ashram? Or is she referring to a spiritual home?

June 9, 1978

I have been seeing everything around me in a new way. As I walk I notice sticks on the ground point in a direction, and the shape of the moss on the rocks gives me a message. I find myself following the signs. I am no longer the ordinary wife and mother from back East. I have moved into a different kind of awareness that is totally new to me.

This evening as I sit alone near the beach prayer room and reflect, I shift into a series of waking-dream experiences. I seem to be guided by an inner voice that instructs me, and opens my understanding to a level of being I have never known before. I feel a sense of oneness with the universe and I follow the guidance of this part of me throughout the night.

By early morning, I am sitting on a rock looking toward the northeast, where I can see a huge ponderosa pine etched against the night sky, softened by the first glow of the sunrise. I see the Cosmic Mother in the form of the giant tree, silhouetted against the sky, about to give birth. She bends gracefully toward the east, her back turned slightly away from me to shelter her birth process. She seems to be blessing the world, as one by one the clouds in the soft pastel sky emerge from her womb and drift off eastward. I see in the clouds symbols from my dreams and other shapes suggesting meanings I don't understand. I am so moved by the monumental beauty of it that it brings tears, but I cannot draw my gaze away. I am viewing my own creative birth process, a mystery opening and expanding before my eyes.

The light heralds the approach of the sun and everything seems to be crowned in light. I look up in gratitude for this beautiful vision, and as the shapes slowly dissolve I feel the first drops of rain on my upturned face.

I am filled with the wonder of what I have been shown. But after these experiences I feel lost, unsure of what I need to do to honour them. I move as though in a dream. There is a feeling of a universal significance that I am experiencing, larger than me. But I finally realize I am getting confused and wandering away from my centre. I need to come back to the grounding of what I am learning in the teachings here at the Ashram. I return to my room. I have barely seen Dawn lately, as I have been in my own world.

June 11, 1978

The Ten Days is almost over. I feel like a sponge that has soaked up so much it is heavy. My inner critic is at work again; questions, questions. I need time to let all that has happened seep into the core of my inner being. I have experienced natural things around me imbued with new meaning. My inner sight has opened up. My mind has been expanding into new levels ever since the course started but I can't put into words much of what I experience. I have much to take back with me and study, not only the experiences I had but also what I learned in the classes – the mantra and dreams and my Life Seal drawings.[1]

Dawn has had her own experience of the course but she will be flying back without me. Swami Radha has suggested I stay longer to take some time to get grounded and do some reflecting.

June 13, 1978

I have an appointment with Swami Radha at Many Mansions.[2] I meet with her in a room downstairs and one of the residents takes notes. I

---

1 Life Seals® is a workshop in which participants draw symbols representing various aspects of themselves.

2 Many Mansions is the house that Swami Radha lived in at the Ashram. The name comes from the Bible. In the King James version, in the book of John, verse 2, chapter 14, Jesus says, "In my Father's house are many mansions..." implying there are many ways to achieve enlightenment or Christ consciousness, and that the Divine turns no one away.

want to ask her about the waking-dream experiences that made me feel I was one with the universe.

She gets right to the point. "This is not the time to go to the universe – stay with Peggy White![3] It is like trying to advertise ten years in advance that you are going to give a concert as a professional pianist before you have even learned how to play or have done any practising. *Keep your feet on the ground!*" Her directness makes me sit up and take notice of every word she says. She means business.

"In regard to any experience you have, write it down as soon as possible, including the date and circumstances. Recall in as great detail as you can, include what you feel the message is and any insights you have. Analyze the symbols and what each one means to you. You must really work with the material that emerges; otherwise it is nothing more than an internal movie.

"Work on your own material as intensely as you can. It is your own decision how quickly to move into the Light. Also give yourself time to adjust. You have fifty-four years to sort through in your housecleaning. Do not expect to have everything back in its proper place in a week. It is important to clarify things in your own head as much as possible first."

This is helpful and makes me feel more accepting of myself. I realize how much I have been judging myself. I ask, "Swami Radha, you mentioned an emotional backlog that built up over the years. Do you have any suggestions about how I should deal with this?"

She recommends that I take the three-month Yoga Development Course[4] at the Ashram in January. Then she startles me by saying, "I suggest you write a paper on 'How Do I Lie?' and 'What Games Do I Play?' Pretending to agree when you don't and then letting resentment build up until it explodes. It is not why you lie, but the ways in which you lie. It is important to write these papers so I can see how much you

---

3   My name before I took *sanyas* was Margaret White. Peggy is a diminutive of Margaret.

4   The Yoga Development Course is a concentrated, three-month course of self-investigation and spiritual development given annually at the Ashram in January.

understand. If you do not understand, you will not recognize self-deception. Try to see clearly how you lie, and what games you are playing, with husband, children, friends, relatives. This honesty will form the foundation on which advice can be given to remove the trap."

Does she see something in me I don't know about? I feel unsettled inside as she says this, which is a clue that I need to look at myself more deeply.

Then she talks about domination in women. "Learn to see how you dominate others. Many women disguise their steel fist in a velvet glove and are not nearly as helpless as they seem. If you can discover even ten percent of your own self-will and bring it under control, you will have come a long way. But be sure you also discover your strengths to give balance. Learn how to bring out these strengths in the most positive way.

"Some years there are lemons here and some years there are oranges. But both have vitamin C."

I ask her how I can prepare for the Yoga Development Course (YDC). She refers me to the course reading list and suggests I buy some of the books and highlight passages as I read.

"You know," she says, "people who come to the Ashram more than once show by their actions that they want to do something positive in their lives. I try to kindle that Divine spark within until it can bring the Light of understanding into all areas. People often say that I am a very demanding teacher. This is true. If the best is not demanded from people, they will not develop. The keys are to be honest and to have humility, gratitude, sincerity, and to do selfless service. Both Jesus and the Buddha had a former prostitute as one of their most devoted disciples. The lukewarm people who don't truly put their energy into anything don't get anywhere. The measurement of the depths will reveal the heights that can be reached."

Her eyes soften as she brings her hands together at her heart in the gesture of *namaste*.[5] "May the Light within you continue to grow and

---

5   In the gesture of *namaste,* the palms are placed together at the heart centre. Swami Radha described it as meaning, "The Divine in me greets the Divine in you."

illuminate your path into Divine Light. *Hari Om.*"

I thank her and leave with my mind buzzing and my emotions churning. I will start writing the papers she suggested, although I must say my initial reaction is shock – I am an honest person and I don't lie! And I certainly don't try to dominate people! But already I am aware of some subtle ways I lie, such as covering up my feelings and saying I am fine when I am not.

I remember what she said about how far the depths reveal the heights that can be reached. After my early morning waking-dream experience of last week, I fell into a confused state of mind that detracted from the essence and the meaning of the experience. And yet I know there is something of great value there that I need to reclaim and honour.

June 14, 1978

As soon as I start writing the paper on lying, I see how many ways I am being dishonest, and the paper on games is just as revealing.

When I make excuses I am usually not telling the truth, as when I don't want to accept an invitation but don't want to give the real reason. I list many points that often relate to pride or insecurity or laziness. I had no idea I was doing this in so many areas of my life. The paper on playing games reveals many ways that I play the martyr game. There is making noise in the kitchen banging pots around and slamming cupboard doors so people will be aware of the work I am doing and perhaps feel sorry for me. Then there is dropping down on the couch with a big sigh showing how tired I am from all the work I have to do. It goes on and on and I feel embarrassed at how little thought I have given to this manipulating behaviour. I want to change.

June 20, 1978

Summer solstice, a turning point and time to leave the Ashram. At 5:00 a.m. I go to the prayer room. The light of the sun's first rays in the east touches the top of the western mountains where the full moon has already disappeared. I spend some time in stillness and then walk along the lakeshore, experiencing a feeling of peace in my farewell. Occasionally a fish jumps, a gentle splash in the still waters, a loon calls farther up the lake, and in the woods a woodpecker hammers at a tree. I want to carry the spirit of this magical time with me.

During breakfast Swami Radha sends a message that she has read my papers on lying and games and is delighted with my insights. She says to be patient. Her words of encouragement are a gift I can take back with me.

I think grace must be operating in my life to bring this experience at the Ashram. I know I had done a certain amount of preparation but there was still some element needed that I could not supply myself – grace, a gift from the Divine. And for this gift I am grateful.

July 15, 1978 Philadelphia

I have been back home in Philadelphia for almost a month and my old life now seems like my "other" life. After all I have learned at the Ashram, it has been such a challenge to come back to this life. However, I am reading the books to prepare for the YDC and that helps me keep in touch with my Ashram experience.

I am excited to receive a note from Swami Radha.

"You did some very good work while you were here, and it is my prayer for you that you will continue with sincerity and goodwill to put in the same amount of effort now that you are home again.

"Remember that when your children were first learning to walk they would sometimes lose their balance and fall, perhaps even hurting their little bottoms quite painfully. But they picked themselves up and tried again until they could move with skill and confidence. So it is with spiritual babies – the first steps are often quite painful and difficult, but with perseverance and goodwill the results will soon become apparent. While you were here God answered a prayer not to let you go without a spiritual gift, which seems to have been the gift of insight. Keep it growing!"

I feel like the spiritual baby who also sees wonder in the newness of experiences and sometimes the input is overwhelming. So I am letting it all settle inside me, using the practices I have learned. When Dawn visits, we relive our time at the Ashram and do the practices together. When I am here alone, the practices have become an important part of my day. In the Divine Light Invocation I connect with the Ashram, visualizing the Light spreading out across the US and into Canada to the Ashram. I also had a dream in which Swami Radha shows me how being in the Light gives more control over life events and relationships.

December 22, 1978

I sent Swami Radha a Christmas card of a print I made of Mary reflecting by a pool and receive a card from her that touches me deeply.

"Reflection is indeed a key that will unlock many deep mysteries with time and patience. I would like to convey a message to you that was given to me by my Guru, Swami Sivananda. In 1955 at my first visit to his Ashram in Rishikesh, he told me that it was the privilege of some people to help in the Divine work, but that this opportunity is not given to everyone. The blessings that are given for your own attempts to assist in the work will bring joy to your heart, and this understanding might be considered your spiritual Christmas present. In Divine friendship, Swami Radha."

How will I help in the Divine work and what does it mean that this opportunity is not given to everyone? Does it mean that some people don't make the decision to assist or that the opportunity is not even presented? It seems to put my life in a bigger perspective.

three | THE YOGA DEVELOPMENT COURSE

January 15, 1979 Yasodhara Ashram

I am doing something I have always wanted to do – every day attending a school that teaches me all the spiritual disciplines. I realize this is a strong desire I have had for a long time, and here at the Yoga Development Course, it is coming true.

Today the group is on silence – not speaking except in class. As I bring my lunch back to my room I meet another student on the way. Our eyes meet and there is a special feeling in that meeting. As I walk the rest of the way I am aware of the energy withdrawing from that aggressive impatient part of me. It is like surrender, an inner surrender, an inner acceptance. I am where I am. I am what I am. I have an overwhelming feeling of gratitude to Swami Radha and to everyone who is so patiently and gently helping my inner flower to unfold. It is a very humbling experience.

Swami Radha is away teaching in the US for a couple of months, and I am a bit disappointed that she is not here. But I have a friendly and good-natured roommate, and I feel a sense of wonder in finding what I have always wished for.

February 1, 1979

As the weeks go by, the teachings of yoga open up and I begin to see myself in a new way as some of the protective coverings dissolve. I go over my papers to review what I have learned in the course so far. There is so much. I am amused at my paper on chanting the mantra for two hours. I started out eager, expecting great things. Before long I found myself battling with a resistant and impatient mind, a body full of aches and pains, and emotions building into frustration.

At one point I drifted into a half-trance state. I heard voices and saw smiling faces asking, "Do you think she's learning anything?" And many nodding heads giving an affirmative reply.

I wondered what was happening to me. Where was the uplifting experience I was supposed to have? I felt tears coming, and I told myself, "All you need to do is surrender." I had only ten minutes left. Suddenly my fingers on the harmonium[1] were playing softly and slowly. I was chanting quietly with a feeling of humility. The turmoil dissolved. A new feeling of peace took over. Obviously this was only a small first step. What a powerful experience of the importance of surrender!

February 21, 1979

The Straight Walk[2] workshop reveals another experience of surrender, but quite a different one. Each person is given a space to walk in and observe what thoughts come to mind. In the downstairs hallway, I am given instructions to walk from there (the far end of the hall) to here (the near end). I misunderstand the instructions and instead of walking back and forth I only walk that one direction, but the experience I have is amazing.

I walk slowly with a feeling of majesty and reverence. I am one of the magi approaching the Christ child. I have no gift to offer. I am almost to the door at the end of the hall. Oh, but this is not a real door.

---

1 A harmonium is a table-top hand pump-organ.
2 The Straight Walk® is a walking meditation workshop.

This door is my own limitations blocking me. I know it will open and disappear as soon as I go down on my knees. Yes, even the magi knelt before the Christ child. I am in the pose of surrender, a feeling of reverence, gratitude and peace.

In class we work with the symbols of this experience. My walk clearly shows my direction, yet the limitations I place on myself are blocking me. The magi aspect of me knows what to do. Will I be able to carry this into my life when I leave the Ashram?

March 27, 1979

The end of the course is near. Swami Radha is back from teaching in the US and she comes to our class. She talks about many things, including the Rose Ceremony[3] at the end of the course. I am completely captured by her flow of ideas and I sense her inspiration rising to fill the room. Her talk about dignity resonates with me.

"You should not allow anybody to injure your dignity. You have an inherent right to your dignity. But often what you are protecting is just ego. You have the right to protect your dignity and the knowing of the Light within, however faintly or naively it is expressed. It's of no less value just because it's naively expressed. A diamond is a diamond, even if it's not polished. Remember that. If you can't break your bad habit of poor self-image, nevertheless consider yourself a diamond in the process of being polished."

I am so glad she has mentioned this about dignity. In my marriage there have been situations where my dignity has been injured. When I was teaching, my husband told me not to work full-time as it would put us in the next income bracket, resulting in higher taxes. His words belittled what meant a lot to me on a deeper level. But when these situations arise I tend to think it's just my ego that is hurt. However, there is a different feeling between dignity and ego, a different resonance inside.

3 The Rose Ceremony is a ritual of personal commitment. See Swami Sivananda Radha, *The Rose Ceremony* (Spokane, WA: timeless books, 2004).

She also has some strong words to say about responsibility. "We have to live with awareness. We have to know what we are doing. We have to be in a waking state and not be sleepwalkers. You have to take responsibility for yourself – for your actions, for your thinking, for your reactions. And then if things get tough, you can ask the Divine to assist you. Put simply: God will work with you, never for you." That is an affirmation I can put up on the wall in my room. I want to remember those words.

March 29, 1979

Swami Radha meets with us to answer written questions we submitted earlier.

She picks up a small piece of paper and looks at it and immediately puts it aside. "If you don't have the respect to write your question legibly on a decent piece of paper, then I am not going to bother to answer."

The next question is mine, on Kundalini energy, and she speaks at length about it. I want to know if the energy we use in daily life is Kundalini energy.

"Kundalini energy is neutral energy. All energy is neutral, including electricity. When energy is used in such manifestations as sexual and creative expression, this is not necessarily Kundalini. Kundalini is a latent energy. It is not the energy that most people are using.

"You have to decide what you want to do with the energy available. It does not have to find expression in sex only; express it in art, in handicraft. Don't scatter your sexual energy, this most precious essence of your being, just for self-gratification. We are not born to have a climax. That is not the purpose of life. And you cannot say, 'Well, since I had Kundalini, I am sexually so much more capable.' That's not true at all. Your inhibition has been removed, that is all."

Swami Radha is so open and direct talking about sex. I was brought up in the era when sex was not talked about. I know my parents had a very loving relationship, but I never thought about it in terms of sex. And I have never thought about sex in terms of levels of consciousness. I must give this more thought.

"When you emerge from the instinctual worlds and become conscious, become truly human, you begin to understand that the urge to obey the instincts has been very forceful in the past, but you could perhaps stem the tide. With that understanding you become considerate of others. You must be willing to take responsibility for absolutely everything you do. You can't put it onto somebody else. Nobody has the right to have pleasure, self-gratification, at the expense of somebody else.

"If babies are born as an unwanted byproduct of sex, don't blame Kundalini. Nature wants to play its part and has provided the rules."

What does she mean by this? My husband and I certainly wanted the three children we had. We expressed our caring for each other through sex. But then I began to have a glimmer of the spiritual level that was possible. What happens if only one partner senses this?

She finishes her talk with some of her very down-to-earth advice. "Let's live in the here and now and do the work at hand. You have plenty to do right now. Start. Do the work. Don't waste time trying to figure out how well you did. Just do it."

Yes, I need to just do it. I have much to work with and ponder on when I get back to Philadelphia.

March 30, 1979

The course ends with the Rose Ceremony. This evening the room becomes charged with the vibrations of the mantra as the twenty-two members of our class chant *Hari Om*. Swami Radha is seated at the front looking radiant in her sari. A few people at a time approach her to receive a rose and then kneel at a low table with a bowl of water in the centre. Carefully, they put the rose petals in the water one at a time, each one representing a pair of opposites to be offered back to the Divine.

When my turn comes I kneel in front of Swami Radha. Her dark brown eyes meet mine with an intensity that goes right through me, as if she is asking: What is your commitment? What are you willing to sacrifice? She hands me a single red rose and I feel tears well up from a deep unknown place. Kneeling at the bowl, I place the rose petals in the water, silently releasing my resistance and my acceptance, my ignorance and my wisdom, and all my other pairs of opposites, in exchange for the love and compassion of the Divine. I feel no hesitation in placing the centre of the rose in the bowl with the petals. This gesture is a symbol of my commitment to the spiritual path, to my higher self and to Swami Radha's work. It comes as an outgrowth of the last three months and of everything in my life leading up to this point.

I have developed a deeper understanding of the scope of Swami Radha's teachings, and also a deep appreciation of what she has made available to us in the West. I know now that Hatha Yoga is a spiritual practice and the *asanas* become a prayer to the Divine. I have discovered that my body holds old memories or attitudes from my past. By doing reflections in the poses, I am able to release some of the holdings.

These are totally new concepts to me and I want to pursue further levels of her teachings in Hatha Yoga, dreams, and especially Kundalini, which covers so many areas of self-investigation and spiritual practice. I have just started laying a good foundation, and I feel ready to make a deeper commitment to Swami Radha and her work.

April 5, 1979

It is time for me to leave the Ashram. I visit Swami Radha to say goodbye and ask her to sign my Kundalini book.[4]

She looks at me with a serious expression and says, "Peggy is a little girl's name. She cannot do the work that needs to be done, but Margaret can." And she writes, "To Margaret – Kundalini, the path of understanding, love, joy, and awareness toward the Light, Swami Radha." I take this to mean that she wants me to use my given name of Margaret and put aside the old name of Peggy. It's like moving into a new part of myself.

As we embrace I say to her, "I will be back." In my heart there is no doubt about that. She smiles. "I know you will."

---

4 Swami Sivananda Radha, *Kundalini Yoga for the West* (Spokane, WA: timeless books, 1978/2004).

four | THE MOTHER

September 6, 1979 Philadelphia

I wonder why so much happens all at once. Since the YDC I feel as if everything has been speeded up. I have decided to move out on my own and have been looking for a place to move into but it is so hard to find something that is simple and still cheerful. Places with a single room are drab and depressing, not the kind of place I want to live in. I feel so unsure and alone. Is this what I really want to do?

September 19, 1979

The most amazing thing has happened. I have been feeling so discouraged about finding a place to live. Nothing has been working out. So yesterday I sat down and thought about my ideal apartment. I figured out the rent I could afford, then visualized a space in an older house with a room for yoga classes and a yard with shade trees. When I looked in the local paper, there it was – the exact rent and the description of what I had envisioned.

I called and was the first person to inquire so I went right over. I could hardly believe my good fortune as it was far more than I had asked for. I took the lease and said I would read it over and let the owner know my decision before the weekend. I do feel this will be the place for me but I have to let the owner know right away. She wants to open it up to other people.

September 20, 1979

I haven't told anyone about the place I have found and my mother-in-law, Mother White, doesn't know about our decision to separate. She seems to be slowly withdrawing, getting weaker, unable to communicate. Perhaps I don't need to tell her. Why upset her at this stage of her life?

I visit her in the nursing home, knowing that she is approaching the end. I hold her hand, softly telling her to look for the Light and that will protect her. She looks so fragile, not at all like the strong-willed, feisty woman I knew in earlier times. When I say goodbye, her eyes are closed but there is a soft smile on her face. I squeeze her hand gently and tiptoe out.

After leaving the nursing home I go back to the apartment for another look to make sure my mind hadn't blown it up out of proportion. When I see it again I know it is just right and will suit my purpose. But I end up in the tiny kitchen feeling totally alone. In just a couple of weeks, this will be my home. How will I face the next part of my life? My mind is racing and I am scared.

I gaze out the window that overlooks the property across the street where some Catholic nuns live. My eyes are drawn to a statue of Mary in the garden, her hands turned outward in a gesture of giving. She looks so serene and I feel she is giving me a message of compassion, sending me her protection. Tears of gratitude well up and I know in that moment that the Divine is with me. She will care for me.

I have learned from this entire experience how important it is for me to state clearly what I need. I have to make a decision and be specific. When I do this then the Divine can work with me.

From there, I go to teach my first Hatha class in a community centre an hour away. I do the Divine Light Invocation and put my class in the Light as part of the preparation. I also see my mother-in-law protected in the Light. The class gets underway and is going well when there is a knock on the door. A woman comes to tell me that my husband has called. My mother-in-law has just passed away and I am wanted at the house. But it has only been a few hours since I said goodbye to her. How could she have gone so fast? I feel a deep sadness mingled with a sense of relief that she is released from the physical limitations that frustrated her. I give thanks for those last moments with her. It all seems like a dream as I excuse the class and leave.

I feel such turmoil as I drive back to be with my husband. I have not yet told him about the apartment but this is not the time to add to his emotional burdens. I feel in a quandary. Should I go through with the decision to leave? It seems like the wrong time and I feel so uncertain. But then I clearly hear a strong knowing part of me, "If you don't do it now, you will never do it. You have to take action." I know in my heart that this is true. Tomorrow I'll go to the nursing home to collect Mother White's belongings, and I'll stop at the apartment to give the signed lease to the owner. Then it will be done!

October 10, 1979

I feel alone yet excited at the sense of freedom of being in my own apartment. I know independence will not be easy. I will have to call on the strong, clear part of myself from now on. But I have the practices and the teachings from Swami Radha and I am in a new place in myself.

I enjoy my tiny apartment kitchen where I can look out at the statue of Mary across the street. She is part of my day as I repeat the Divine Mother prayer to her and ask for her blessings.

> O Divine Mother
> May all my speech and idle talk be mantra
> All actions of my hands be mudra
> All eating and drinking be the offering of oblations unto thee
> All lying down prostrations before thee
> May all pleasures be as dedicating my entire self unto thee
> May everything I do be taken as thy worship

I feel so fortunate to have this place where I can work on my YDC book reports and do my practices. I even have an empty space for teaching small classes.

I take time from setting up the apartment to go through the dream journals that I have kept for many years. While looking for a particular dream that came up in the YDC, I come upon one from ten years ago that I completely forgot about. I am amazed as I read it:

February 20, 1969: I have written a book. I give it to Gina Cerminara to bless at some kind of ceremony. She takes it and does a ritual, then hands the book back to me. She asks me where I was born. I go blank. I can't remember where I was born. A voice says, "Don't you remember? You were born in British Columbia." "Yes, of course," I reply, "I always had BC after my name."

Gina Cerminara is connected to the Cayce work and has written a book on reincarnation. Did this dream refer to a past life connection? I had this dream nine years before I went to the Ashram. In a sense, I feel like I was born in British Columbia. A new life started on that first visit to the Ashram in BC. All those years ago, maybe a part of me knew about my future, a part of me that has no limitations of linear time.

January 10, 1980

Feeling lonely today. I go out for a walk in the cold crisp air and realize that I am getting in touch with a new aspect of myself as a woman. No longer a sense of being interpreted through a man. Without being in the shadow of a family or husband or children, I have the opportunity to be a woman – no old roles, no covers, no demands. Just being myself.

I am lonely if I am caught in emotions of neediness and looking outside myself for support. Being alone allows me to connect with my inner strength and the Divine source. I can be in a crowd of people and be alone, and I can be in a crowd of people and feel lonely. The former feels strong while the latter makes me insecure.

I return from my walk with an uplifting sense of power. I am alone but I don't have to feel lonely. The choice is mine.

January 15, 1980

I have a test today when my husband calls and asks me out for dinner. I accept. No harm in that. We go to a favourite restaurant and the evening begins to take on the excitement of a date. We have not seen each other for a while and our difficulties become blurred in illusions about the past. It wasn't so bad. Perhaps we can make it, after all. I can feel my resolve weakening.

Then his beeper goes off, calling him to a fire in the city. He is one of the volunteer drivers for the fire department. "Come on, I have to go. I'll drop you off at your place. It sounds like a major fire." I wake up to reality and recall the numerous times this has happened in the past. I know this is not what I want in my life.

Emotional reactions are softened through the passing of time. It is obvious that I need to accept our differences and that it is important for us to follow our separate paths as friends. As Swami Radha says, "You are much more the master of your own destiny than you realize. If you don't want to be lonely in your approach to the Divine, you have to decide to allow yourself to be caught in the net of Radha and Krishna. It is personality aspects that keep you separated and bring about that powerful sense of loneliness. But you can change that."

February 2, 1980 Philadelphia

I dream of the two great mother figures of my life:

I have brought some friends to a place where Swami Radha is. She comes outside and greets them warmly. My mother kisses her and then says in a smiling, blank kind of way, "How nice to see you. Who are you?" I think, "Oh, no. How could she make such a dumb mistake." Swami Radha goes over to a table to talk with some people. After a few minutes, she gets up to leave, as she has a lot to do. I walk past her. She reaches out her hand to me and I touch it, maintaining contact right to the tips of our fingers as I pass by. We smile at each other.

In the dream, I think my mother's question, "Who are you?" is an embarrassing mistake. But on waking I know that "Who are you?" is life's biggest question. It is the major question of the YDC, urging us to explore who we really are. My mother is asking the question I need to ponder daily. There are so many levels to uncover.

May 3, 1980

My mother died several days ago. She made the transition peacefully in her sleep and even though I have been preparing for her death for quite awhile, it's still a shock. The various members of my family are here and today we have a simple memorial service for her. The minister reads a section from the Book of Proverbs that reminds me of her: "Strength and dignity are her clothing, and she laughs at the time to come. She opens her mouth with wisdom, and the teaching of kindness is on her tongue. Many women have done excellently, but you surpass them all."

After the service I do the Divine Light Invocation for her. I see a beautiful image of her as a young woman with long hair standing in the centre of a blue flame. I know she is at peace now. I feel gratitude for her life, for the time I had with her. She taught me so much. I am glad that she has finally moved into the Light, but she leaves an empty space behind.

May 11, 1980 Toronto

I am in Toronto with my friend, Virginia, who organized our Cayce Search for God group over ten years ago. We are attending a Life Seals workshop and I am excited to see Swami Radha again. We were instructed to draw and colour symbols of aspects of ourselves in advance, and mount them on a larger sheet of paper or cardboard. I have mounted my drawings on black cardboard, as the store didn't have any white and I wanted something sturdy to withstand the traveling.

The group gathers in a room in the yoga centre. I greet Swami Radha and she welcomes Virginia and me. In my session she tells me,

"The black cardboard background shows the unknown part of the Divine, affirming the mystery of God. There will always be things you will not understand about the Godhead. Now about the whole shape of your life seal – you rounded the top of the piece of cardboard, so it looks like a door to a tabernacle, a holy space." I am surprised, as I hadn't thought of this. It gives another perspective to my Life Seal.

I have drawn a tree to symbolize the part of me that is growing, producing fruit to share with others. She says, "Now turn it upside down with its roots firmly established in heaven. This brings fruit of a different kind."

"But, Swami Radha," I ask her, "what about the energy from the Earth, the importance of Mother Earth?"

"Margaret, that is for the first three levels or chakras, but it is necessary to go beyond that. We don't want to be stuck on the Earth level. We want to move beyond the third level of consciousness." So with the roots of the upside-down tree in Heaven, I would be established firmly in Divine inspiration.

She looks at my drawing of balance scales held in my hand, symbolizing the difficulty I have making decisions. "You know, Margaret, your indecision may be viewed as the skill of holding things in balance until the Divine opens the doors showing you the direction in which to move." I am glad to hear this, as it gives me a different perspective and I can be more patient.

She closes, saying, "I am very pleased about the progress you have made over the two years, though there is still more to be done. But if you have done this much in two years, just think what you can do in the next two years."

Her words about making progress bring up feelings about the past year since taking the YDC, of all the difficulties, yet at the same time a sense of things falling into place. The Divine seemed to move in harmony with me once I made a conscious choice about the direction of my life, the choice to follow Swami Radha's teachings. My husband and I decided to separate, and then I found the right apartment because I was clear about what I was looking for. My mother-in-law and then my mother passed away within seven months of each other. All of this has set me free. I have no further feelings of responsibility weighing me down. The unfinished business in this part of my life is resolved.

November 19, 1980 Philadelphia

Swami Radha is here in Philadelphia on a surprise visit! She is staying at my apartment and I am so thrilled to have her here. She has kindly offered to meet with some friends who have expressed interest in having contact with her. And some of the members of the former Cayce group want to see her again. She answers questions and talks on many different subjects, just allowing ideas to come up through the questions.

On our way to a talk she gave to a local group, we drive past the house I lived in with my husband. She says, "That looks like a lovely house. Why would you leave that?" I know she has asked this to find out where I really am at in my life. I am sure of the answer and reply, "Why would I stay? There was no longer any meaning to being there."

December 30, 1980

After Swami Radha left, I sent her a thank you note, and asked her a question that had been on my mind: "While at the Ashram, I heard many people call you Mataji. I felt a resonance with this name, and my heart tells me to call you Mataji, but I am not sure if this is all right." Today I receive a card with her response. I am deeply moved by what she says.

"The meaning behind someone calling me Mataji has to do with the first stages of a spiritual commitment to me as a spiritual teacher. Mataji in fact means revered mother or spiritual mother. It includes the willingness to listen to and take action on the spiritual instructions that I give, and to have an attitude of service to the work for which I stand. There is personal responsibility in calling me Mataji that is deeper than addressing me as Swami Radha. If you can accept that responsibility, then it would be fine for you to call me Mataji. In Divine Friendship, Mataji."

This brings me into a deeper place in my relationship with her as my spiritual teacher. There is no waffling now, just moving forward.

five | COMING HOME

May 22, 1981 Yasodhara Ashram

Dawn and I have finally arrived at the Ashram. It was a long trip but we took turns driving and read aloud from the *Ramayana* epic. This made the trip so much easier. We finished the story on the last day. I am so excited, ecstatic to be here. I feel as if I truly have come home. We will be here for a year! Swami Radha invites us to visit after supper. We brainstorm ideas about possibly starting a centre in the Philadelphia area and she seems to be quite discouraging on one hand, but willing to lend support on the other.

We also talk about what I will be doing after I get settled in.[1] I am interested in working in the bookstore, but she mentions the kitchen as a place to start.

July 23, 1981

I have adjusted to the work schedule and seem to be doing all right, although I do need a rest in the afternoon. I like being able to run down to the lake on hot days to have a dip in the cool water. One day I meet Swami Radha on my way up to the guest lodge after a morning

---

1 The Yasodhara Ashram is a Karma Yoga ashram. This means that one of the main practices is practical work as selfless service.

in the kitchen. She asks me how I am getting along. I tell her, "I am really happy to be here but when I am in the kitchen my legs and feet get tired, I guess from standing so much."

I expect some sympathy but she tells me directly, "You have to do the Divine Light Invocation and really fill your feet and legs with Light right up to the top of your head. Your tiredness is from your attitude. You can change that."

Another thing she mentions is not trying to please everyone. In helping to make others aware, you can't always be nice. She compares the spiritual path to taking off in a rocket. A tremendous effort is needed to get beyond the pull of the Earth, but once out beyond this…!

July 24, 1981

After the talk with Swami Radha yesterday, when I am a bit anxious about another morning of Karma Yoga in the kitchen I remember her reminder about the Light. I try to keep my tiredness in a joyful frame of mind.

I work quietly with Ed in the kitchen. My obsession with wanting to do it just right comes through, but Ed helps me to see that I worry too much. I definitely do not get as tired today even though I work just as hard. So attitude and focusing are both important. The other residents suggest that I delegate more in the kitchen and think of doing a good job without getting hung up on being perfect.

Swami Radha says, "Most of our ideas about perfection come from our upbringing. They are just our preferences about what sort of things we like. These have nothing to do with spiritual perfection. Never seek perfection for recognition. Seek it only in the service of the Most High."

August 2, 1981

This year is Mataji's twenty-fifth anniversary of becoming a swami. Her *sanyas* initiation was February 2, 1956, but we are celebrating it in August because it is a more convenient time for most people to come. It is exciting to see many people from both Canada and the US arriving to be part of the celebration. I get up at 6:00 a.m. to pick raspberries. It is a lovely day with the sun just starting to break through the trees, the two young heifers watching me and mooing occasionally, the chickens squawking their accomplishment of egg-laying. I stop picking at 7:00, and we all get together to chant mantra for an hour in honour of Swami Radha.

In the afternoon there is a tea on the Many Mansions lawn and I see Swami Radha by the fishpond. Her eyes sparkle and the sun shining on her white hair creates a halo of light. She seems so happy. I walk over to greet her. "Mataji, you must be very pleased to see all of these people here at one time."

"You know, Margaret, this celebration has given me a different perspective on my work. It has compressed all the years together so I can see what has been accomplished. It is quite surprising to me to see how many people I have been connected with. When I am working with a certain person I can't think about the others who have gone before; I am too busy in the present moment."

"Well, I'm sure glad you did all the traveling around you did or I wouldn't be here now. But there seem to be people from all over and it shows how many people have been touched by you." I feel I am one of those people. I have such gratitude for finally being a part of the Ashram and having a connection with her.

I am surprised at what she then says about the Ashram. "I have always wanted to prevent the Ashram from growing too large. Most people need structure and aren't able to handle freedom; but I leave people on their own and only the serious ones develop their own system or schedule and stick to it. That is how I keep the Ashram small enough that people don't get lost in the numbers and I can give more individual help."

"Mataji, I don't know how you have the time to do all the things you do. How did you make the Ashram what it is today when you had nothing after your return from India?"

She smiles at me. "When people tell me what a wonderful job I have done building the Ashram, I make it clear that many people have helped, contributing much energy and money, so really the Ashram belongs not to me but to many people." I am touched by her humility. Some leaders take all the credit for the work that many others have contributed to, but she is really honest. She makes me feel that even the small donations I sent to her were appreciated. I want to show her I can be responsible and stick to what I have set in motion.

October 7, 1981

I am reciting Robert Frost's "Stopping by a Woods on a Snowy Evening." The last lines suggest I have a mission: "But I have promises to keep/ And miles to go before I sleep/ And miles to go before I sleep."

Swami Radha has told me she knows what my mission in life is, but says I have to discover it for myself.

At lunch today she asks me to come over for a visit in the afternoon. We talk about the history of the Ashram property and my connection here. She implies that I have previously experienced this place. A psychic told her she had lived here in 10,000 BCE and had been part of establishing a square temple at the beginning of the teachings. Now is the conclusion, and she is making plans to build a round temple[2] on this site. If I have lived here previously, that might explain the waking dream I had in 1978 on my first visit. It could have been old memories and feelings surfacing.

December 11, 1981

Over the fall months I have worked in the kitchen, the garden, and cleaning the guest lodge. Mataji told me to write papers about what I

---

2 Swami Radha had a series of dream experiences that started in her teens about seeing a small round temple, looking inside and seeing showers of light. The foundation of the temple at the Ashram, a realization of her visions, was laid in 1965, but other building projects were necessary and no further work was done until 1989 when construction began again.

learned and give them to her. This is to prepare me in case she sends me to start a centre in the East. I have done that and she seems satisfied.

I have found the kitchen to be the best learning, as it brings back the many years of doing things my way. Today, I interject my suggestions when someone is making the soup instead of focusing on what I am doing with real care and attention. I forget that it is all an offering back to the Divine. I just have to get myself out of the way.

This evening Mataji sits beside me as I am finishing dessert. She asks me some questions and then tells me to always write down my understanding of any conversation I have with her. That way I won't forget.

"You need to be aware, Margaret, of how you want to serve the Divine on your own terms. You must learn to truly turn yourself over to the Divine. Thy will be done; ask to be shown what to do and then sit back and observe, wait. Don't move too fast. Ask that the doors be opened for the next step. If it is just temptation, ask that they be closed. And you can ask for confirmation in dreams.

"This will help you to learn to listen. Insights will come this way. Also they will come through chanting so your mantra practice is important as well."

These points of awareness are really instructions for me to follow. I am receiving them from her personally and I feel very grateful that she takes the time to help me. She really touches a place inside when she says, "Remember you may not be saying, 'Yes, but...' out loud, but are you still saying it in your head? Letting go of old concepts and becoming aware of new ways of looking at something is a freedom." How did she know I do this? Like I am arguing with her in my head instead of being open to something new.

Then she reminds me of the demands of spiritual life.

"In the early years I had to combine the work here with my practices as I often didn't have time for both. Many times I only got four or five hours of sleep."

I am amazed and reply, "I don't think I could do that."

"You could if you think of your connection with the Divine as a love affair."

When I go back to my room I think about what she said. I give that last statement much thought, sorting out rationalizations, my own experience, and the realization that my understanding may be limited. From my experience at the level where I am now, I find that if I am working hard physically during the day, my body needs enough sleep to keep body-mind healthy. If my love affair with the Divine is a timeless ongoing process, then I carry it with me day and night, sleeping and awake. If I have the right attitude, my life, no matter what I am doing, is an offering to the Most High. I realize this may be true on a certain level, but there is more I may not understand. She is helping me to stretch my concepts about everything to overcome my limitations.

Christmas Day, 1981

This is my first Christmas away from my family. I thought I would be homesick but I have been enjoying every part of our celebration here. There is much joy, with a wide range of activities from chanting and singing Christmas music to skits and opening presents. Mataji gives me a beautiful ivory cross, quite old. She looks at me intensely to get my total attention, and says, "The cross does not mean just the crucifixion. It also means the crossroads at the heart chakra. Do you want to go on just being a nicer person, or do you want to go the whole way?" This question startles me. It puts my life very clearly on the line. I am not sure what going the whole way means, but it calls for a much deeper commitment.

April 20, 1982

My understanding of Karma Yoga (selfless service) at the Ashram is deepening, but I still face my old patterns – pushing myself, getting obsessive about certain areas of work, finding it difficult to allow time for personal practices. The attitude I need to do Karma Yoga is just the opposite. I want to do my best without my perfectionism making me take on responsibility that isn't mine. I want to do what needs to be done because it is there to do – no rewards, no praise, no expectations. I am doing it for the Divine. Perfectionism comes from my ego and limits my ability to make each project an offering to the Divine. I fear not doing well or not being acceptable. I have always underrated my abilities, but this really doesn't matter if I simply offer my best.

Mataji accepts me as I am. Recently she gave me a scarab ring and told me to wear it all the time. It is made from a stone that is common in Egypt and looks like turquoise. It is large but is strangely comfortable and just fits the ring finger of my left hand. Wearing it feels like a way of connecting to something deep inside that has to do with Egypt. I don't know what it is, but I have had dreams about Egypt and am attracted to its history and its art.

Swami Radha is such an amazing person. She is honest about her shortcomings, and talks openly about her struggles to move beyond them. It is obvious her connection to the Divine and her ability to surrender to that Divine power are the keys to both her strength and her total commitment to do what her Guru asked of her here in the West.

June 23, 1982 Philadelphia

Dawn and I have come back East for a month. I need to settle some personal business. I went to the cottage at the Jersey shore where I have spent so many happy and peaceful hours, and was surprised to discover there is no longer any attachment. I don't have a sense of belonging anywhere here. During this time I have missed the Ashram and everyone there. I feel the Ashram is my home now and I want to live there.

I receive a note from Mataji regarding my future work: "I am looking forward to having you back because I am delighted with your drawings and invite you to make many more for the Hatha book."[3] A dream come true! I have always felt something missing about my art

---

3   Swami Sivananda Radha, *Hatha Yoga: The Hidden Language* (Spokane, WA: timeless books, 1987/2006).

training – a purpose, a meaning. Why was I doing those paintings and lithographs?

I had a talk with Mataji before I left to come east and she asked me about my art training. She was interested to know that I had followed through on my education. I was in my second year of a fine arts degree at Wellesley College when I left to get married. Once my children were all in school, I returned to college, attending one with a good art program near where we lived. Eventually, I received my bachelor's degree in art in 1965. Then, because I wanted to teach art to schoolchildren, I did a master's in education, which I received in 1971. By that time I had been teaching for three years.

What I was missing, however, was a purpose for my artwork. I wasn't satisfied just doing it for myself. While stimulating children to reach their own creative potential was rewarding, I yearned for something more. That something more is the heart connection.

July 31, 1982

I give some thought today to my fifty-eighth birthday. I review the year and see I have developed a lot, making progress on letting go of a past that was no longer working for me, developing a new identity for myself. It seems to be such a slow painful change while it is going on. I open myself to those forces that are attuned to my growth, assisting me to work on my inner development. I ask for guidance so that I may make the right decisions. I offer my thanks for all that I have received. Much has been given me. Everything changes. I must move on, never holding onto what is no longer needed.

I have made an effort to live according to my inner ideals. For the coming year I want to continue to develop inwardly. I want to be open and aware. I don't want to fool myself, to rationalize things, to cover up or mask my true feelings so that I have difficulty understanding what is going on. May I be cleansed and cleared so that love and joy flow through me and out to others. May this be my focus for the coming year.

August 29, 1982 Yasodhara Ashram

I sit down by the lake – early morning, utter stillness. An occasional splash of a fish jumping out of the water; a brief cry of an osprey, then silence. I absorb the feeling of peace and tranquility. No longer the anxiety I experienced back East, the sense of not belonging. I am at home here, content. Is it because there is a kind of protection here? Is it the loving support and companionship of those who have similar ideals to mine? But do I have the ability to maintain a high level of involvement in my spiritual practice? Can I do what is necessary to keep growing? This life, this direction, is the most deeply satisfying. If I just devote myself to it, do my best, my inner Goddess will let me know. Listen, listen, listen.

six | ART AS SPIRITUAL PRACTICE

September 2, 1982 Yasodhara Ashram

When I am settled into the Ashram a few days after my return from Philadelphia, Mataji invites me over to Many Mansions to work on the drawings for her Hatha Yoga book. She tells me to use her library for my research.

"Go through the books and get acquainted with what is there. Then you can make little sketches and tape them where they belong in the margins of the manuscript. That is a good way to start putting your ideas down."

It is great fun, not work at all. I have no distractions except looking out the window at the lake and mountains, where the mood changes with the shifting patterns of light. Swami Radha's desk is next to my table and we work quietly, her focus helping me to be single-pointed. She gets up to find a book and stops to give me a hug. Why I am so blessed?

November 5, 1982

Mataji and I have breakfast together. She talks to me about my life before I came to the Ashram.

"To survive you have to move on. It does no good to hold onto your hurts and your pretences and your ego." She looks at me intensely and her words go right into me. I tell her about the war years: the uncertainty of the future, the message to grab your happiness while you can. I was in college and my fiancé was going to the war in the Pacific. So, in the pressure of the times, we got married.

"This is the wheel of life," she says. "Once you set something in motion you cannot stop it without repercussions. In marriage you set something in motion; in family life there is a commitment." Her words are so clear but I didn't have that clarity then, as I moved into the life of a mother and the keeper of our home. I had put something in motion and it had to play out.

December 15, 1982

I have a sense of peace within me. I am living to the utmost in the present moment, enjoying and appreciating everything I have been given. I try not to dwell in the past and I have a feeling the future will take care of itself. My dedication to the teachings, to the yogic way of life, is very firm, but I no longer feel I have a need to call the shots, so to speak. I will let my Divine Committee take care of what is right. Putting all my attention on what I am doing now will allow me to get more out of the present time and my life will have more richness and quality.

December 27, 1982

I am sitting with Swami Radha in front of an altar at her place. My picture of the Botticelli Madonna hangs on the wall above as a focus. To the right of this is a large painting that is not very well executed, but it has a certain power. It shows a woman sitting in a chair. As I look at the picture more closely I see there is a stream of light issuing from her forefinger, which is outstretched and pointing. She is sitting in profile looking toward the left side of the picture. It is in various shades of blue.

I doze off for a while and when I wake up I see that Swami Radha has moved the picture of the woman over so that it is the focus of the altar.

There is a lovely simplicity augmented by the power of the painting. I real-ize it is a painting of Swami Radha when she was younger. The Light that streams from her finger now seems to be coming from around a paintbrush she is holding. She is painting a picture.

Swami Radha now sits quietly in front of the picture looking at it. I realize I have been here a long time and it is time for me to leave. I get up and say goodbye.

Many feelings emerge as I awake. The dream is mostly in blue, a spiritual colour for me. I am moved by the images of Swami Radha and the Light. I know there is a message for me about using art as a spiritual practice. I take time to reflect on the dream, using Swami Radha's method of dream work. I write down my associations for the main words in the dream and use these connections to discover what the meaning of the dream is for me now. This dream has so much in it that I write many pages, yet I still feel there is a sense of mystery that perhaps I will never completely understand. There may be more levels to unfold, but I summarize what I see at this time.

I am in a space in myself that is spiritually oriented and focused on the area of worship. I am considering three approaches: the Ashram approach as manifested in the altar, the prayer room; the traditional Christian approach rooted in my upbringing (the Botticelli Madonna); a more original personal approach inspired by Swami Radha and given focus through channeling of the Light. It doesn't have to be perfect (I am not perfect!). This latter way is emphasized. Meaning can be ab-stracted in further refinements, simplifying. I don't need to be limited by the outer form.

I am amazed at the depth of meanings of the many symbols. The focus of the first part is the painting of the blue woman, of Swami Radha as a young woman, but of course on one level she represents an aspect of me. At first she is pointing with light, but after I lose awareness (falling asleep), I wake up to another level, and I see that the Light streams from a paintbrush as she paints a picture. The essence of my goal in art is to give expression to the Light. And Swami Radha, representing my higher self, is the inspiration for this. All of this takes place in front of an altar showing the spiritual direction that means so much to me.

December 29, 1982

I go to the prayer room to draw the Botticelli Madonna from my dream. Then I go to Many Mansions to have breakfast with Mataji. After breakfast she goes over my dream with me and gives me some good pointers. Her main concern is that I will not honour the changes I have made and will be drawn back to my old ways. I want to assure her of my commitment through my sincerity and my actions.

February 24, 1983

I am working on the Hatha book when Mataji calls me on the intercom. "Margaret, do you have time to give me a treatment this morning? My neck and shoulder seem to have knots in them." She chuckles and adds, "Someone must be giving me a pain in the neck! But I am aware that sometimes people send a plea for help in the night. I wake up and don't know what happened, but I can feel it in my body."

I am so glad I followed my urge to get massage training before I came to the Ashram. At the time, I was interested in a number of kinds of bodywork and was quite enthusiastic about this particular massage course, even though I had no plans to practise massage professionally. Mataji questioned me carefully about my training and told me to write a paper on massage and the sense of touch. I did a lot of reflection, relating this to the Kundalini system.

She also talked about people getting into bodywork to satisfy an ego need. They may want to help, but they may also unconsciously want the personal satisfaction of healing someone. It can be a very subtle thing. Also, it is important to keep the person and myself in the Light so I am not giving of my own energy or taking energy from the other person. The more I work with her guidance, the more I see how the massage treatments are a spiritual practice.

Soon after I begin the massage, she falls asleep. Her body seems to need the release from tension caused by her involvement with so many aspects of the Ashram and so many people. From time to time I look out the window to see sunlight dancing on the lake. This reminds me to keep connecting with the Light within. I finish with a foot massage and stand quietly at the end of the table until she stirs and wakes up, smiling.

"I fell asleep, didn't I?"

"Yes, it has been about an hour."

"That long? It shows I feel comfortable with you. And you never seem to drain me. I feel much better now." She stretches and sits up. She seems in no hurry to get back to her work so we sit together on the floor facing each other. She mentions pain and the sense of touch. She has had to deal with much pain over the years.

"The pain in our life often outweighs the joy." Then she adds, "You never know how much time you have left. Learn all you can now because it is harder in the other dimensions. And use all of your five senses. Bring them into balance."

May 12, 1983

Dawn and I have to go back to Philadelphia to be interviewed about immigrating to Canada and to pack up our belongings for the move. The residents are doing a practice of ten Divine Light Invocations a day, so we have decided to do this on our trip. It is a wonderful way to travel in the Light. We stop in rest areas and do the Invocation in the parking lot or sometimes we do it in a bathroom when we stop for gas. I feel it is a real protection for us.

May 16, 1983 Philadelphia

We are staying with a mutual friend who lives in a big old house just outside of Philadelphia. It is an intense time, as I am taking action to deal with the last details of my former life. There is a lot to sort through.

While packing, I come upon a project I had done in high school in 1940. I had researched the life of the Buddha and illustrated it with some watercolour sketches. As I turn the pages I wonder why I saved it all these years. Suddenly I come to a picture of the wife of the Buddha, Yasodhara! I am stunned, but there it is written at the bottom of the page. Did a part of me know?

I continue sorting and am startled to find a drawing I did when I was at Wellesley College during a sketching trip my art class made to the Boston Museum of Fine Arts. I paused in front of a strange little figure dancing on the head of a snake. I read the name Krishna, but it meant nothing to me. I knew nothing about Krishna, the beloved of Radha, the name of my future guru. I made a sketch, put it aside and then forgot about it. I wonder why these two pictures are the only ones I saved.

Many emotions arise as I try to decide what to take and what to give away or sell. I won't have much room at the Ashram and it is time to let go of the accumulation of many years, even some things that still have meaning for me. But this is a strong symbolic message that I am making a big change in my life and it is important to honour that.

I am glad that I can give things to family members, knowing that they will be appreciated. However, my daughters and son don't like the idea of my moving so far away. But I have to make sacrifices if I am going to lead the kind of life that is important to me.

July 21, 1983

My interview went well. This is one occasion when my age is a bonus; I am retiring to Canada so there's no concern about me taking a job from a Canadian. Dawn, being twenty years younger, has a different status and will have to return to the States from time to time.

August 9, 1983 Yasodhara Ashram

Dawn and I arrive back home at the Ashram tired but happy. Mataji greets us with hugs and much warmth. She tells me I will be in the Garden Room in Many Mansions. I am thrilled to be here and I feel such gratitude as I stand in the centre of the room looking all around. It is a lovely, spacious place with an open view of the lake and mountains. There will be room for my furniture when it arrives.

I feel it is a great honour to be in Swami Radha's house. It brings me a step closer to her in a practical way but also in a symbolic way. It tells me something about the decisions I have had to make and the benefits of following my heart. I am grateful to the Divine for leading me here. I used to feel there was something missing in my life, but now there is a sense of fullness. May I be worthy to follow the next phase of my life.

seven | TOWARD MANTRA INITIATION

June 1, 1984 Yasodhara Ashram

I am doing some drawings at the table next to the desk where Mataji is working. It is a good system and it helps to have her presence close by.

Today she asks about the waking dream experience that I had on my first visit to the Ashram. I give her what I wrote then. She reads it over and seems quite astounded. "There is very interesting symbolism here. But you know, it takes ten years to develop a solid spiritual base, so you have no time to lose." Before we can discuss it further she is called away. That always seems to happen.

June 6, 1984

After morning Hatha I have breakfast with Mataji in the screen house. She says she wants me to learn office procedures and bookkeeping.

"You are a good organizer and manager and you have a way with people."

I pause to let this sink in, as I don't think of myself in those terms. "I will try to do whatever I am given to do."

She mentions again the possibility of my establishing a teaching centre in the East. This concerns me; I doubt if I can do it and I have done so much to move here to be at the Ashram. Of course, Mataji often brainstorms ideas that do not come to pass, so I should not worry about something that could change tomorrow.

She continues, "I will point things out to you, not as criticism, but just to let you know for the purpose of teaching others. I want you to tell me if something goes strongly against your grain." That seems very fair. But some things might go against my grain and yet be what I need to learn. I must discriminate between a strong preference I have and a fundamental principle I need to learn.

After supper I give Mataji a foot massage, and she tells me to write papers on renunciation and initiation, as it is important to start thinking about what a mantra initiation means to me. This sounds serious. As I understand it, mantra initiation will link Swami Radha and me over many lifetimes. She will undertake to guide me to self-realization; and I promise to work toward this however long it takes. Am I ready for this? Do I really understand the depth of commitment necessary to do this?

She continues, "After a mantra initiation, there is a two-year preparation for *sanyas* initiation when I have complete control of what you do. I tell you what to read and what practices to do; I may ask to read your dreams and diary to see where you need help. I decide what work you do. If there is something you want to do before you start, that is okay, but the idea is to cut out distractions for the two years. Also if there are any personality aspects of mine that annoy you it is important to tell me so we can discuss it. I am telling you this to let you know what to expect. We need to be clear with each other."

I still feel nowhere near ready for initiation. I feel I need to take one step at a time.

I remember right after my Yoga Development Course Swami Radha asked a lot of people at the Ashram to write a paper on mantra initiation. I look up the paper that I wrote then and am surprised to find it expresses ideas about initiation that are still true for me even now.

I consider the word "initiate" as a verb. It implies starting something. My Guru is the instrument for establishing a new start for me as a neophyte. A new relationship is created requiring mutual responsibility and understanding. Open communication takes place. She undertakes the guidance of my spiritual progress; I, as an aspirant, become responsible for following the directions of her as my Guru and for upholding her teachings. A special bond is formed that transcends the present lifetime.

Initiation implies instruction. I must listen carefully and follow instructions – both are activities that require surrender. To listen carefully I must surrender my preconceived ideas, my desire to interject my own ideas or replies, my self-importance; I also must surrender the inverted ego that denies my sense of self-worth and thus blocks the ability to listen honestly.

First, I need to develop the ability to listen to others without interrupting. Next, I have to control mental back-talk while listening to others (planning a reply before they even finish). Then comes the surrender of really listening to my Guru and eventually understanding the meaning behind her words. Finally, I learn to listen to the subtle voice of the Most High revealed in unexpected or unexplained ways. This kind of listening requires discrimination, as my mind can create what I desire, simply as compensation or for self-gratification. I must be absolutely sincere and honest about my motives. Otherwise my imagination may create fantasies that I could mistake for the real thing.

Surrender is involved also in following instructions. I experience this in the Ashram kitchen, where I often have to do things in a way contrary to my experience or my preferences. I have learned simply to surrender to the situation. When emotions come into play, true listening is impaired – I hear only what I want to hear. How can I follow instructions if I have not listened carefully and set aside emotional reactions, preconceived ideas and mental background noise?

Withholding judgement is also required. I may be asked to do something that seems irrational, inefficient, beyond my capabilities, or questionable. Instead of reacting or resisting immediately, I need to think about it and perhaps even try to do it. If I have an honest question, I need to get clarification. My Guru may say or do something that seems to be unfair or even harsh, but a deeper look shows there is a learning experience for me. I certainly have to be clear.

June 24, 1984

This morning the lake is perfectly still with reflections of the mountains mirrored in such a way that they seem to be reaching down into the depths of the water. The sky is clear with only a few scattered clouds. The first impressions I have as I walk out of the door are the fresh early morning smells and the songs of the birds that seem more evident at this time of day. I walk down to the lake through the woods and sit on a large rock absorbing the wonder of the day. Then I stand up and do the Divine Light Invocation in the brilliance of the sun. A perfect way to start my day.

After breakfast by the fishpond, Swami Radha gives advice on mantra practice. "Wake up with the Divine Light mantra and say it aloud. Keep saying it aloud to drown out all the mental noise. In your mantra practice if your voice needs to warm up, do the lion pose. Stick your tongue way out. This will help your throat to relax. Sing a scale and then go one note higher than is comfortable for you. And remember it is important to chant out loud." I will try these exercises to help me reach the high notes of *Hari Om*.

July 15, 1984

In *satsang*[1] in the prayer room I am facing the lake and am aware of the shifting light of the sun setting behind the mountains. During chanting I keep my eyes open to watch the sun and ponder its cycles of rising, reaching its zenith and setting. The light holds my attention as it gradually fades away.

---

1 *Satsang* is a service honouring the Divine during which devotional songs, referred to as *bhajans*, may be sung, an inspiring talk given, and a mantra chanted.

When I go to say goodnight to Mataji the subject of Egypt comes up. She tells me that she has had a strong impression several times that we had a life in Egypt together. She says, "I have good feelings about it and once I wanted to just blurt out, 'What was your name?' to see if you would respond without thinking. But there were too many people around so I didn't." I wish I had some memory about our connection but I don't.

July 21, 1984

Swami Radha has several residents over for breakfast and talks to us about a number of things. She tells us not to clutter our minds with unnecessary information. "Keep a file of the kinds of things you can look up so you can keep your mind free for more important things. And beware of asking questions just to keep the conversation going. This is unnecessary questioning – idle curiosity. Don't waste your time on this. Remember that taking one step at a time may be all right occasionally, but if you move too slowly it can be a kind of protection – and if you hesitate too long, the Divine might clobber you."

I need to take this in for myself. It took me eleven years to get to the Ashram after first meeting her in 1967!

"I am often asked why I don't make things easier for people," she says. "But someone has to maintain high standards and be serious for those people who don't want just entertainment and who want to go deeper in themselves."

She always inspires me to bring in my own inspiration and enthusiasm to the dream class I am teaching. She encourages me to challenge people to work hard, and perhaps they will be fired up to put more effort into their dream work. I see how being a good teacher is like building a house – start at the base and work up, adding, refining and developing the various parts. I need time and experience to do this.

August 12, 1984

I wake up to thunder rumbling across the lake where dark clouds hover ominously above the mountains. Yet the sun shines on the mountaintops, creating an eerie light. Gradually the storm moves north up the lake. I get such a startling view from my room.

Today Swami Radha talks about the need to have images to focus on. "Remember this is part of the process toward focusing on the Light and then on the formless. Without that process it is like someone saying, 'Here is the alphabet, now here are the sentences. Go write a treatise on surgery and next week you can perform an operation.' That would be ridiculous.

"When I objected to the images of deities Sivananda told me to watch my mind. Then I discovered a whole parade of images, some going back to my fears connected with Nazi Germany. I realized they were like tapes playing over and over. It was necessary to replace them consciously with images of a spiritual nature."

August 15, 1984

I finish giving Mataji a massage, and she asks with a smile, "Would you like something special to happen on Gurudev Sivananda's birthday[2]?"

At first my mind is blank and then it suddenly comes to me: my MANTRA INITIATION! I can hardly believe it. I am close to tears. I start to say I am not ready, but realize that is not being grateful. I look at her with a jumble of feelings and thoughts.

"Oh, Mataji, I don't know what to say. I do trust you to know if I am ready or not. It is such a surprise."

She replies gently, "Take time to reflect and think about it. And keep the mantra going as much as you can." She doesn't give me any other instructions except not to say anything to anyone about it. I tuck

---

2 Swami Sivananda's birthday is September 8th and is chosen as a special date for initiations.

it into my inner mental closet where I treasure it as a special secret. Sivananda's birthday is September 8th, only three weeks away. I am feeling very excited but peaceful at the same time.

August 18, 1984

I am with Mataji and we are laughing. She gives me a kiss on my cheek and there is a feeling of closeness.

This dream is another sign of my connection with Mataji on an inner level. That is important because the mantra initiation involves a very deep commitment. We will be karmically connected for the future and this is a big boost for me on my spiritual journey. She will help me get to the goal of self-realization. I feel grateful and humble and realize the responsibility this involves on my part.

In my morning Hatha practice I really focus on an awareness of the mantra filling the cells of my body. I am able to hold the sitting forward bend longer than usual and feel my upper body gradually merging with the lower part.

September 8, 1984

This is a big day, Swami Sivananda's birthday and my mantra initiation! There is chanting for his birthday first thing in the morning and a dance presentation after lunch followed by a guru *puja*[3] later. It has been inspiring and a perfect preparation for my mantra initiation tonight. Mataji comes to my room and tells me not to eat much supper. We talk about who will be coming to my ceremony. Dawn will be one of the seven people supporting me.

My initiation is held before the altar in the prayer room in Many Mansions. The large picture of Sivananda is there, still garlanded from the *puja*. Mataji brings me into her private room and hands me a white cotton sari as a symbol of a new beginning, the purity of a new life. I am so glad she helps me to put it on, as I am excited and a bit ner-

---

3 *Puja* means "worship." Guru *puja* is a ceremony honouring the guru as the Divine.

vous. My hands are shaking so she pins the folds over my shoulder. She smiles at me and gives me a hug and leads me back into the next room where the others are chanting.

We sit in front of the altar and she instructs me first to honour Sivananda by prostrating to his picture. As I bow down I feel a deep connection to him and the lineage.[4] I become so immersed in the feelings I lose all sense of time until I feel Swami Radha's gentle touch on my shoulder reminding me to come back up. As the ceremony proceeds I feel my heart opening up and my body responding even though I do not understand fully the depth of meaning. I need time to let it sink in.

At the end Mataji looks intensely at me and says, "The ceremony is simple and short. It is the work that is long; but I think you know that." She embraces me and I feel that I am giving myself to her and the work, making a commitment to a higher purpose. She says, "Now you can dedicate yourself to going to the Light, not just now and then, but all the time so you will make it to the Light in this lifetime." We look long and deeply into one another's eyes. It is as if we are communicating on a level beyond words. Yes, Mataji, I will take the initiation to my heart and keep my commitment to you clear and true. I am blessed to have received this sacred rite that links us together in a relationship for lifetimes to come. May I be worthy of her trust in me.

She gives me the candle and the *prasad*[5] that is left and I return to my room to reflect on the significance of the initiation and the power of the mantra. I think of the mantra as a silver thread linking the various parts of my life, and stitching the inner parts of myself into a new pattern. It weaves into my day, leading me from one activity to another.

---

4   There are twelve orders of *sanyas* in India. One of them is named for Saraswati, the goddess of wisdom and the arts: music, poetry, literature, song. Gurudev Sivananda's lineage is of the Saraswati order.

5   *Prasad* means "grace." Here, it is the sweet that is handed around and consumed at *satsang*. It has many symbolic meanings, including the sweetness of the gift of life and nourishment provided on all levels by the Divine.

It touches the cells of my body and illuminates dark corners inside. So I let the mantra weave a pattern containing all that needs to be expressed. Then I release it into space. Where does it go? Does it disappear? No matter, it has woven a cloak of Light around me that brings me a feeling of peace.

September 9, 1984

I take time to work on dreams, to chant and reflect. When I do the Divine Light Invocation and visualize Mataji in the Light, I feel a surge of vibration. Another time I experience everything as huge, spacious and powerful.

I take a walk in the woods and feel a weird combination of sensations. I realize I am feeling a lot of things that cannot be expressed in words. Perhaps it is best to give them time to filter down into me.

I wear my white sari to *satsang* and am able to concentrate better than usual. Mataji gives us a good pep talk. I am the last one to *pranam*[6] to her and we have a big hug. She tells me to keep the sari. Wear it to all *satsang*s and Ashram functions and when I do any spiritual practices alone.

September 13, 1984

I give Mataji a foot massage and afterward she says, "You are a very special lady. You bring quality into everything you do for me." That is encouraging, as I am not always sure that I am doing the right thing. But I do feel we have a strong bond.

Afterward I think about what it means to bring quality into what I do. It has to do with being aware and not doing things mechanically. It is also being connected to the Light or thinking about the Divine in some way. I wasn't very aware in earlier times as I was often functioning from my emotional centre. It wasn't until I got into the Cayce group

---

6   A *pranam* is a bow of respect given to the guru, an altar, or any representation of the Divine.

and then Swami Radha's work that I learned how my mind and emotions interfere with clarity and awareness.

December 25, 1984

After supper on Christmas Eve we have our Christmas party at Many Mansions. We light candles and put them on the altar as we say a prayer for the coming year. The residents each give Swami Radha a card with the gift of a spiritual practice dedicated to her for a certain length of time. She takes all the little cards and puts them on the altar in front of the statue of Tara, the goddess of compassion. This is a more personal and thoughtful gift than buying her something. It also brings us all together on a deeper level.

On Christmas day Swami Radha inspires us with her *satsang* talk about how we can give birth to our inner Divine child through our dreams. She tells us some of her dreams and some stories about the Christ child and Krishna. They were both born in humble settings, the Christ child in a cave or stable and Krishna in prison where the evil King Kamsa had confined the baby's mother and father. But Krishna and the Christ child both escaped the evil forces, King Kamsa and Herod. This is because they had a greater destiny.

Swami Radha says the miraculous stories of baby Krishna's amazing feats are just like the wondrous things our own spiritual baby can do. She mentions the young boy Krishna as the butter thief. He is mischievous and climbs up to reach the pots of butter hanging from the ceiling. He steals the butter to give to his friends and they giggle as they gobble it down, smearing it all over their faces. But we, too, steal the cream and milk from the cow to nourish our bodies. Swami Radha says it is all right as long as we use our bodies as a temple of the Most High.

eight | CHANGES

March 14, 1985 Yasodhara Ashram

Mataji is leaving on a trip to visit one of the Radha centres[1] connected to her work. As a group of residents gather to say goodbye, she talks about making changes in our lives. "See yourselves as chicks in the egg. When the food is all gone, the only thing left to do is break the shell and emerge." She laughs. "That is your Easter gift to yourselves!" Then off she goes and we turn to the quiet and emptiness without her. It is particularly noticeable to me because I live in Many Mansions where her presence is so vital. But even when she is gone I feel some part of her is still here.

April 11, 1985

In my dream I wake up from a dream and am telling someone about it. Then I actually wake up.

I think about how my dreams and waking life connect. If I can wake up from the dream state to the so-called waking state, can I also wake up from the waking state to a super-waking state of reality? Is my life as much of a dream in terms of reality as my dreams are? Why do I sleep/dream? One answer may be that in sleep I sink back into a

---

1   Swami Radha founded a number of centres dedicated to the teachings of yoga in cities in Canada, the US and the UK.

deep state that brings me to a union with Divine consciousness but I am not aware of it. I spend a third of my life sleeping in that deep state and I need that time to keep me in touch with the Divine source. If I can consciously begin to contact that state of being, then I don't need as much sleep. This is why Swami Radha keeps emphasizing ways to maintain a contact with the Divine in daily life.

Swami Radha told me once that it is a good thing we spend as much time sleeping as we do or the world would be even more chaotic.

May 19, 1985

I am talking with Mataji. She tells me to start doing Likhita Japa[2] *again. The dream gives me really specific instructions.*

This kind of communication is helpful when Swami Radha is not here. She has been away for a couple of months, but she will be coming home soon. I purchase a nice journal in the bookstore to use for writing the mantra. But with the plain paper I can also make images with the writing, using pens of different colours. This is an inspiring way to do a spiritual practice and it connects my love of the Divine with my interest in art.

May 29, 1985

Mataji is back. I join her in the sunroom with one of the younger male residents. He has a mind of his own, but he also has a real sweet side. She has mentioned previously that we must not hold him in an old image. He needs some extra help and I observe how she relates to him. She discusses plans for him to do some work in one of the Radha centres. I can see him start to lighten and glow.

She explains to him carefully, "I am not critical of you but I might have to question you if I don't understand something. That is different from criticism. You see, I am an authority in my area and you are an

---

2 *Japa* is the repetition of mantra that may be silent, whispered, spoken, sung or written. *Likhita Japa* is the practice of writing the mantra.

authority in your area." He beams. By approaching him this way, she has helped him to respect her and to respect himself. I appreciate Mataji letting me learn this way about working with people. I see that she is firm when necessary and is gentle when that is needed.

September 19, 1985

Mataji's health is a continuing major concern. Changes and directions have been on my mind. In what direction is the Ashram going? These have been critical times with the uncertainty of the commitments of a couple of residents. It must have an effect on Mataji and her health. I know my own overall direction. The uncertainty of others seems to make me more clear and sure in myself. I want to support Mataji as she has helped me to change my life.

February 12, 1986

I am with a lovely girl child about eight years old. We are running freely over freshly plowed earth, up a slope, laughing, free.

This dream is a real gift. It is a reminder that the part of me that was born eight years ago at my first visit to the Ashram is really with me. She brings much joy and lightness. Last June I had a similar dream in which I was playing with Swami Radha's seven-year-old daughter. (She doesn't have a daughter, so it is obviously part of me.) Both dreams tell me that a new spiritual child was born in me at my first visit to the Ashram in 1978. My unconscious seems able to keep track of the important dates and time frames in my life and present dreams that affirm the connections.

July 12, 1986

Mataji has been traveling a lot this year, staying at some of the Radha centres. She has just returned and she looks great. When she meets with us tonight, she gives us a sobering thought about the explosion of the Challenger space shuttle. "You have to remember that millions of people were watching this on TV. The Divine used this situation to get a message across. Look at it as Krishna's *lila*[3]. It is like baby Krishna pulling over the butter pot and breaking it in an instant. You never know when your time is up. And what have you done with your life? We think we are so aware but we are not. We are all hypnotized." She has us all thinking seriously about this. The atmosphere in the room is very heavy as everyone ponders about the bigger picture.

But then Mataji tells a story on a lighter note and the mood shifts. We end up laughing. She has often said we have to look seriously at what is going on around us, but we must not get fixated on the trauma and become identified with the negative. We have to look deeper at the whole picture.

July 14, 1986

We are very fortunate this summer to have Mataji meeting with a group of us to explain her method of teaching and how she wants Hatha Yoga presented. She gives a very intense introduction on the ethics of teaching. Then she assigns a paper for us to write on ethics and what we intend to do with what we learn. She is concerned about people who leave and then teach their own thing as if it were coming from the Ashram; or use the Ashram material for their own commercial benefit. She feels that anyone who gets training at the Ashram has a responsibility to keep in touch with us and to give something back for what they have received.

July 17, 1986

Today she asks us to write about our own experience of *Tadasana*, the Mountain pose. I write about seeing concentric circles as I went deeper into the pose. It was strange and I couldn't connect it with anything. Then later in class Swami Radha mentions concentric circles in a new

---

3 *Lila*, pronounced "leela," is dance or play. The interaction between the manifest and the unmanifest – creation and its creator – is sometimes portrayed as a dance between the two.

picture she has put up in the prayer room in Many Mansions. Then the connection seems amazing. For me, it has to do with stages of moving closer to the Divine through the poses.

When we go through all our papers on *Tadasana* in class, Swami Radha tells us we have not gone deep enough. I am puzzled. I haven't had experiences in *Tadasana* on the spiritual level, so how can I write about it? Maybe I just have to go deeper with the level I have experienced.

July 21, 1986

After having time to reflect and do more writing, a group of us meet to discuss *Tadasana*. We stand in the pose and then talk about some back problems and what the psychological implications are. For each person it is different. My back is too straight with too much tuck of the tailbone. Most people feel it is a kind of protection. It makes sense because I do feel exposed when I create more of a curve in my back. I am protective about some things, so I guess I could write about that. Is it something from my past I can let go of now?

These classes are giving us a much clearer understanding of Swami Radha's approach to Hatha and the teachings in general. We will no longer be inviting outside teachers to present classes at the Ashram, as this could confuse things. Also, this intense training is preparing us for when she is not here.

November 6, 1986

A faithful servant is rewarded by "the master" for his loyalty. He has been given a place of his own. I am told it is down the hill in the meadow. I can hear the sound of hammering as the building is going on. But later when I am shown his place it seems to be part of the master's house. There are a couple of large rooms that have been partitioned off. The faithful servant feels this is too much, but the master says he is very grateful for his servant's loyalty and he wants him to have it. He even feels that he, the master, should help build it.

This dream has the flavour of a parable from the Bible. It seems to be saying there is a loyal servant in me who is rewarded with a place very close to the master or Lord. I am reminded of Jesus telling his disciples he will prepare a place for them. On one level I see this as preparing me for death or moving into a closer relationship with the Divine. It is an unusual dream – intimate yet distanced by being a story. It touches me on a deep level.

January 8, 1987

After breakfast, while I am sitting with Mataji and a couple of others, she starts talking about teaching. "Be sure you do the Divine Light Invocation after every class and put the students in the Light to make up for any lack of understanding you may have had or to fill any needs you were not able to provide.

"In classes if people don't address their pride they will never be straightforward and will not be trusted by others. They will cover up and protect their pride. This distorts everything." She looks intensely at us, then adds, "Of course, this goes for you as well."

She turns to me and talks about the Divine setting me free. She says I would never have gone for self-realization as long as I was in a comfortable marriage. That is true. Of course, I am not sure I would call my marriage comfortable toward the end. I finally had to take action. Maybe that whole part of my life was the Divine plan playing out.

January 19, 1987

Mataji decides to have more Hatha classes for the residents to prepare them for teaching. Tonight we have a delightful class with her. She is warm and gentle and full of Light. She certainly emphasizes the spiritualizing of the body, chanting or repeating mantra while doing Hatha so every cell will be affected. I find it difficult to chant out loud, ask myself questions and figure out what is going on in my body all at once. She says you don't have to do all of those. Once you get some insights, wait awhile before investigating further. Each person finds her own way.

What I find helpful is writing reflections about what my body is doing in the pose and then finding out what my mind comes up with. It is amazing what I learn from this. But most of all I like to explore the symbolism. There is much to write about with the tortoise, such as moving slowly into the pose like a tortoise. Also I feel like I am in a shell when my spine is curved over with my hands holding my feet. I have a sense of being deep in the water, safe and protected.

June 20, 1987

When I take the joy I am feeling into my mantra practice, I focus on the idea in the *Puranas*[4] of the three qualities involved in experiencing Krishna. The ancient yogis translated their abstract experience of Krishna into something more literal, giving it form: a blue-grey colour like thick rain clouds, they portrayed as the colour of Krishna's skin; a heavenly sound, they represented as a flute; and sparkling lights, they depicted as jewelry adorning him.

In my practice, the blue seems to emerge out of a sense of mystery. The jewels are like a sparkling halo of stars but with many colours. The mantra is the sound. I wonder about Krishna being unfaithful to Radha and keeping her waiting. But I am able to understand that situation as a more abstract Divine principle. I am asked, "Have I ever let you down?" I experience an immediate feeling of deep love and trust because the Divine has not let me down. I have seen over and over how I have been guided and helped in a very caring way.

July 25, 1987

I awake this morning to the sound of thunder rumbling in the dis-

---

4 The *Puranas* are a set of Hindu scriptures containing stories, legends and hymns about the creation of the universe, the incarnations of God and instructions from various deities.

tance. A dramatic storm is brewing. By the time the weekly Ashram meeting starts there are flashes of lightning, strong winds and loud thunderclaps – all an outer manifestation of the emotional turmoil in the Ashram around another long-term resident who has not been following Ashram guidelines about celibate relationships between men and women. At the meeting it is decided he will take a retreat in a small cabin to give him time to work through his problems.

August 9, 1987

This summer Swami Radha is spending a lot of time sleeping outside in her screened gazebo where a bed has been placed for her. She has not been feeling well and this is how she heals herself. I spend some time with her in the evening and she speaks of Radha and Krishna, telling me things I have not heard before.

"Radha is a vortex of energy that doesn't incarnate but manifests through an individual and when that person dies the energy forms in another vehicle which gives it expression."

I ask, "Does everyone have the potential for the Radha spark within?"

"No. But there might be the possibility for manifesting the ray of a *gopi*[5] who is an emanation of Radha."

I think of how I would like to be a *gopi* who is an emanation of Radha. How do I get to that stage? I guess the best way of finding out is to be with Swami Radha and learn as much as I can by serving her. Then I ask her if there is a vortex of energy that is Mary.

"Yes. It is like wearing the dress of the country you are born in. If you read the texts and books like *God as Mother*[6] and try to really understand them, then you will be given all the knowledge you need."

---

5 *Gopis* and *gopas* are the milkmaids and cowherds among whom Krishna grew up and who became his devotees. Swami Radha used the terms to refer to those who lived and worked in her spiritual community.

6 Cheever Mackenzie Brown, *God as Mother: A Feminine Theology in India* (Hartford, VT: Claude Stark, 1974).

I feel privileged to be with her, but at the same time I feel so far behind. My thinking is so limited and my understanding so narrow. But after being with her I feel energized. I think she was giving me the Light.

September 8, 1987

Today I reflect on the third anniversary of my mantra initiation. I feel that I am at a place in myself where I must go deeper. I have been asked to do things I didn't think I could do, but I have never been given more than I could handle. It wastes energy to worry unnecessarily. The times I have allowed the future to unfold naturally without worrying, without resisting, I have come through all right.

But I must not let my spiritual life drift. I want to put more quality into all that I do. I have been self-centred. I keep losing that feeling of seeing each kind of service I give as an offering to the Divine. I have grumbled inside at times. I have doubted and questioned instead of accepting and surrendering. It is important to remember that when I serve Swami Radha I am serving the Divine. I can make whatever I do a way of serving the Divine.

September 14, 1987

At our resident meeting, Swami Radha mentions she is thinking of introducing new rules for interactions between men and women at the Ashram: there will be no talking to the opposite sex except in work situations and there will be silence at meals. I see how concerned she is about the future of the Ashram. She has to maintain the standards it is founded on and the guidelines have to be clear and upheld. The changes seem extreme but it may take something extraordinary to show how important it is to keep the Ashram on course.

She describes the changes as a *tapas,* which is a discipline or doing a spiritual practice that uses the heat of intensity of purpose to burn away the dross, the impurities and the obstacles that stand in the way of the goal of Liberation. It makes sense, but I feel myself going into sadness and resistance. It seems extreme and contrary to Sivananda's teachings of the middle way. However, I have a choice: I can be resistant and glum and keep the inner nagging critic active or I can make a decision to be a channel of Light and joy. The changes will throw us onto our own inner resources and make us all stronger. I will have to look within and not rely on others to fulfill certain needs or desires. I will not have as much contact with others, so perhaps I will have more time for reflection and inner work.

September 15, 1987

I was awake in the night, restless and thinking about silence at meals: it is important to face my aloneness. I will die alone; it is necessary that I make my connection now with my own Divine source so that I face my death without fear and loneliness. I feel that I do accept myself and I enjoy being alone. But I also enjoy people. Eating in silence I am more aware of my own being. I can be more aware of the nourishment I am receiving from the Divine source in the food and in the silence.

When I let go of the resistance, I feel a sense of lightness. I am being given an opportunity to *be* in a new way, to deepen my commitment to the Divine, to look at how I expend my energy. This switch takes a conscious decision and an act of will, not forcing things but gently looking at a different perspective. It is a privilege to have Swami Radha's example of uncompromising values. She cuts through everything to make a point, especially if it is to clear a path to the Divine. She is taking the Ashram and the residents to a new level of maturity and it is up to us to make it work.

September 19, 1987

I am discovering another side to change. There is the resistance to change, which I was experiencing with the *tapas,* but there is also the desire for change for its own sake, as Swami Radha pointed out to me.

"You have to train yourself to be free from the need to change everything. See if you can resist having to change things around just for the sake of change."

I reply, "But I am experiencing the opposite. I am very contented and comfortable in the Garden Room and don't want to change anything."

"That may be true there, but that doesn't mean you are not critical of other people's dress, hair and habits, and would like to see them change."

This is very true. She is getting at a way my ego manifests. How does she always pinpoint something I need to look at? It is true that I tend to want things to stay the same, but also I do complain at times about the way certain things are done and I think I have a better way. And I am aware of being silently critical of a person's hair or mechanical habits. I need to turn these thoughts inward and look at myself.

"Make a cathedral of consciousness out of all those sand castles," she says as she leaves the room. She is preparing for her trip to Victoria tomorrow.

September 25, 1987

Tonight when I am chanting I notice that the white petunia on my altar is pointed toward the picture of Radha and Krishna, resting against it as if listening for some word from the Divine. It is a charming image, a symbol of really opening myself and listening to the Divine, so I use it as a focus to return to when my mind wanders.

September 27, 1987

Mataji has invited the women residents to visit her in Victoria. I enjoy the drive, going on a trip in the van, releasing the pressures we have been under and relaxing in a lighter frame of mind. I sit in the back with my *mala*[7] in my hand, reciting the mantra silently. On the surface level I am observing what is going on, the singing and talking. But I

---

7   A *mala* is a rosary-like string of 108 prayer beads used in the practice of mantra.

become aware of a deep stirring inside. A realization of the immensity and mystery of the Divine and how I am forcing that limitless indescribable essence of all life and creativity into very human forms that bring it into something so much less than it is. Yet the Divine can be anything. I am moved almost to tears.

I think of the infinite space that has to do with blue. I can only get that sense of awe and mystery when I consider the infinity of the sky. I am in the confines of the van moving through a minute particle of space, but I can look out and be aware of the boundlessness of the beyond. What is closest to me rushes past with speed, almost creating a blur. But it is not moving – I am, like my mind moving so fast it seems like everything around me moves; my life moves, time moves. What is farther away appears to remain still. So if I look past my immediate circumstances to what is further away, more distant, more stable, then the racing stops.

September 29, 1987 Victoria

When we arrive, Mataji greets us warmly. We have had a stopover in Vancouver as she suggested, so we are well rested. She takes us all to an Indian restaurant for dinner and we have a great time with much laughter and telling stories. She is so thoughtful and kind to give us this time away, time to be with her in a different way.

September 30, 1987

At breakfast she talks about initiation. She reminds us that she has asked us the question, "Who would you initiate?" but no one has taken the time or trouble to think deeply and give her an answer. To whom would I give that kind of commitment? It bonds the two souls together and means a responsibility for future lifetimes as well as this lifetime. I wonder if I have that kind of dedication. I admire her courage in taking on this responsibility, as she has been disappointed over and over again by those she has initiated.

October 20, 1987 Yasodhara Ashram

Yesterday my final divorce papers arrived. The divorce has dragged on for so long that most of my reactions have already occurred. It is strange that the papers arrived the same day as a stock market crash. I am not worried about my few investments because no matter what happens I know that Divine Mother has taken care of me so far. I turn to her for my security.

When I sit down to chant this afternoon, feelings of sadness and tears come to the surface. Then I feel as if huge gentle arms embrace me with tender warmth. I feel Divine Mother's protection taking the form of acceptance and compassion. The whole upper part of my body feels the warmth of this embrace. My heart opens and the sadness begins to melt away. My practice goes on for an hour as I release my feelings. Then I decide to have a ritual at the lake to bring a conclusion to my marriage and to let go of the past.

Swami Radha has often mentioned the value of ritual to honour a transition. She suggested making up a little, personal ceremony to release the feelings that need expression. It can be very simple and can incorporate any of the practices.

So I pick two flowers representing the flowering of my two selves, the masculine and feminine within. Then I search the beach for two small stones with meaningful symbols on them, a stone for each of us in our marriage. I repeat the Divine Mother prayer, saying a farewell as I throw the stones and flowers into the lake.

I chant *Hari Om* and ask for a Divine blessing on my ritual. The clouds hang low over the mountains, the wind blows toward the shore, but it isn't cold or ominous. The two flowers float to the surface and wash back in. I stand and do the Divine Light Invocation as a final closing of the ritual. I have been doing an ongoing practice of the Light to release my past and this has given me a sense of letting go in a new way. There is an acceptance of what is.

Turning away, I feel freer than ever before. I walk up through the woods smelling the wet earthy smells and feeling a wonderful sense of gratitude to the Divine for the guidance I have received. To be in this place in my life is a real blessing.

October 26, 1987

A flash of a thought passes through my mind as I realize the date is my wedding anniversary. But I do not have any reaction and my thoughts go to the work today. I realize I have moved beyond attachment.

Christmas Eve 1987

During the night, I held my *mala* in my hand. I dreamt of sending Swami Radha a letter by special delivery, a brown envelope with several things in it. Are these the things I need to talk about with her – or with my higher self?

I can hardly believe it, but my first thoughts on awakening are of taking vows. The idea of being a swami has swept over me. It has been more than three years since my mantra initiation. I have asked my dreams for guidance, but nothing has come through. Yet I feel something is going on inside. It is agonizing because it is not clear. It is as if I have to make a decision and take full responsibility on the conscious level, without any help or guidance from anywhere else. But the ego is part of that level and it doesn't want to give up the status quo. Another part of me knows I have to move on. I long for a sign, some guidance.

February 27, 1988

I sit on the rocks overlooking the lake this afternoon for my mantra practice. It is peaceful and I am alone. I start by repeating the Divine Mother prayer twenty times, and then chant the mantra quietly. When my mind wanders I bring it back to the mantra and the feelings in my body. I am aware of vibrations, mostly lower notes in my abdomen and higher notes in my head.

Afterward I sit quietly. I feel a longing. Am I expecting something to happen? No, longing is different from expectation. It comes from the heart. Suddenly there is a sense of largeness, of space, and a realization that the knowing is right there – or here – and all I have to do is acknowledge it. There is nothing that has to happen, it just is. And it is all the time, only I am not in touch with it. No big fireworks, just a quiet powerful knowing. It is so simple. I watch the sun go down behind the mountain and I give thanks for my day. If this were my last day I would feel okay about my life. The prayer I used to say at bedtime as a child comes to me. I realize that simple little prayer was preparing me for death right from the very beginning:

Now I lay me down to sleep.
I pray the Lord my soul to keep.
If I should die before I wake,
I pray the Lord my soul to take.

nine | COMMITMENT

April 22, 1988 Yasodhara Ashram

Something amazing has happened! I wake up sometime after midnight with my *mala* in my hand thinking intensely about wanting to experience a oneness with the Divine. The whole issue of *sanyas* floods in, a realization that I don't want to miss the opportunity to do all that I can in this lifetime. I experience a feeling of surrender and acceptance; yet there is also a feeling that I don't want to accept *sanyas* for the wrong reasons. It must come from my heart.

These thoughts keep flooding in. I look at the clock; it is one o'clock in the morning. Since this is a good time to chant the *Hari Om* mantra, I sit up in my bed and begin to chant quietly. Gradually an image comes into focus of a woman riding on a lion. What is this? She has many arms and each one holds something. This is wild. I see a sword, a bow and arrows, a spear and something that looks like a shell. Yes, it is a conch shell. She has to be the warrior goddess, Durga. I remember reading something about her in a book of goddesses. As she becomes more clear, I begin to connect with the Divine source in a new way with a feeling of power and reverence.

She is riding a lion – of course, I have to direct my Leo personality tendencies, like pride and wanting to be in control, using them to serve me instead of threatening or overpowering me. I think of her many arms holding the weapons she needs for battling the ego, but she also holds the conch shell. Does she use this to call me, as well as for the call to battle? Is this why I always keep a large conch shell near my altar?

Then I see her killing a demon. She looks so peaceful and calm. I see how strong Durga is – she is able to defeat this demon that must be part of me.

Her image changes and I see her glowing form with two arms reaching out to me; no other arms needed now, no weapons. She opens to embrace me and I come to her, kneeling before her and placing my head on her lap. I am like a child coming to the mother. I feel this experience deep in my cells.

A memory starts to emerge of my daughter Wendy and me on a trip to India in 1972, long before any thought of living at an ashram had entered my mind.

We had our picture taken in front of a temple, standing together with garlands of bright orange marigolds around our necks. A celebration was going on with music playing, people singing, bells ringing and many flowers. We climbed up to a higher vantage point where monkeys were clambering on the railings. We stand near them, looking down on the courtyard below, watching as people crowd into the entrance door. This was a temple honouring the warrior goddess Durga. I didn't know any more about her but she seemed to touch the hearts of the people in the village.

And now, sixteen years later, she has come to me. It seems amazing that I made a connection with her so long ago.

April 24, 1988

Today is a celebration day with reflection and chanting for the twenty-fifth birthday of the Ashram. I imagine a long, straight road leading to the Light. The gurus are in a line walking ahead on this road, back in time but still ahead of me leading the way. I can see the large powerful figure of Swami Sivananda with Swami Radha beside him, showing us the way. The Ashram is a state of mind reflecting the teachings that shine and radiate out like a beacon to light the way.

I follow behind on that long, straight road, but distractions and temptations draw me away. I create obstacles on the road that I then have to surmount. I wander off sometimes and get lost in the forest of my own thoughts. But the Light from the road calls me back, the Light of Swami Radha, Swami Sivananda, the teachings – the Ashram where I have the support and guidance. I pray that I may be a part of that beacon that sustains and guides even as I am sustained and protected.

April 26, 1988

I am really getting into Durga's story. There is a dramatic account in the Devi Mahatmya of the gods calling on her to defeat the demons and when she appears in a blaze of Light they drop to their knees in amazement. I find the battle descriptions too gory. And yet it is important to see the symbolism in how she defeats the enemy.

May 1, 1988 California

We are visiting a student in California. The others go shopping and I have a chance to talk to Mataji about what has been happening with me.

"Can I talk to you about my mantra practice?" I ask. She is sitting alone and it seems a good time to approach her. She nods and beckons me to sit down. "My mantra practice is so inconsistent. It varies from uplifting and inspiring to frustrating, with my mind unable to focus. I get discouraged."

She replies gently, "When you had your first baby didn't your feelings vary between joy and frustration with all the problems as the baby grew and got into things? Don't expect too much. But ask of the mantra that you don't want to be a five-year-old spiritual baby – you want to grow up."

When I mention *sanyas* and the uncertainty of the future, she continues the theme. "When you were born did you know what it would be like to be five years old? When you were five years old, did you know what you would be doing in three years?"

"Mataji, you make it sound so simple and it makes sense. I just need to have faith and let go of expectations, of wanting the security of knowing in advance. But I also am not getting any messages from my dreams and wonder why my unconscious is not giving me clear guidance."

"That can only come after a conscious decision has been made."

She is silent for a while, giving me time to think about what she has said. Then she continues. "The language your unconscious uses to communicate is important. It is important to see how the value of a symbol shifts. The longer and more complicated your dreams are, the more touchy you are; short, direct dreams show where you are. Your dreams will start to have a different quality.

"Try to fall asleep with the mantra; chant a mantra aloud when you are getting ready for bed. Keep it going as you go to sleep. Keep the monkey mind focused and maintain the desire to get the message of the dream; if you don't get it this time you will get it later. How intensely you involve yourself with the dream will make a difference. You can get a lot of very good advice. Sometimes you will have to pray to get the message, and pray that you will be strong enough to take it.

"In your reflection at the end of the day look at how your day was different from your night dream. The study of your dreams must lead you to recognize that your waking state is just another way of dreaming. This will help you to understand your mind, and you will see that day dreams as well as night dreams are very important. The powers that determine our sleep dreams aren't that different from the powers that control waking dreams. The power is neutral. It is coloured by desire and self-will, I want, and the idea that something is due us.

"Nothing is due us," she says as she gets up and walks toward her bedroom. "We owe life."

This is a sobering statement. Is it my self-will that wants confirmation that I am on the right track? Do I harbour the thought that I have made steps to affirm my chosen direction of a spiritual life and therefore I should be given a reward? No, I need to be grateful for what I have been given already without expecting anything more.

May 21, 1988

After my morning Hatha practice I ask Mataji if each Hatha pose has a truth to be discovered. She questions my use of the word truth. "There is a result. You should be so full of passion to have the answer that you will do the pose for a week and not eat until the Divine gives you the answer." She talks about doing the twisting posture while chanting the mantra. "This is to gain control of the vibration of sound in the body and be able to move it anywhere in the body."

Then she speaks about the mind.

"Watch the arising of thoughts – which ones catch your attention? Which pass by? Have you ever watched yourself falling asleep?"

"I've tried but it is too elusive. Repeating the Divine Mother prayer is the closest I have come as I sometimes can remember the last line I was saying before I lost it."

"That is good. It is important to know how your mind works, how you manipulate your mind and how your mind manipulates you. If you criticize someone, as soon as you realize what you have done, put the person in the Light; say something positive. In daily life if things go against your preference, remember you did not come to the Ashram for an easy life, but to take a step toward higher consciousness.

"Knowledge radiates from other sources, as well as those we perceive with our senses. What are those sources? The body is too tangible, too dense to pick them up."

I know this; I have a feeling that my body is too dense. Doing the practices must change this. That is what she did and she encourages us to do the same.

May 29, 1988

This time in California has been a wonderful opportunity for me, as there has been lots of time to talk to Mataji. I don't have my own room and am sleeping in the living room. This morning, she peeked in to check on me. She came in when she saw that I was awake and I made us some coffee. We sip our coffee and look out at a beautiful view of the sunlight sparkling on the ocean waves washing into the shore below. Suddenly she turns to me and says, "You can take even the simplest event of the day and turn it into a way of making a connection with the Divine. Look into your cup of coffee and think, 'This is so dark that I can't see the bottom. When do I create a circumstance that is so dark I can't see the Divine?'

"If thoughts intrude on your mantra practice, such as, 'Should I make coffee for breakfast?' then immediately turn it around to, 'I wonder if Divine Mother likes coffee? Does she like cream in her coffee?' It doesn't even have to make sense just so long as the connection is made. You can use your daily reflection to do this as well. If you do this often enough, eventually you will be remembering the Divine all the time. Then you don't have to meditate three hours a day. The object is to live in the presence of the Divine."

I realize this is how I can use my interfering thoughts in a positive way. Also, when I serve Mataji I can think of this as serving Divine Mother. It is my thought, my attitude that is the important thing.

Then she says, "When you are sitting with me don't think about entertaining me. You can sit quietly and see what thoughts emerge. You can have a little book handy and write them down."

I do what she suggests. For instance, sitting outside and looking at the trees I think, "Every leaf is a prayer to Divine Mother." Looking at the grass: "Every blade of grass is a manifestation of Divine Mother and I just take it all for granted, even walking thoughtlessly on the grass without thinking about stepping on her manifestation."

July 19, 1988 Yasodhara Ashram

Mataji has been ill off and on since returning from California. She has been pushing herself to come to our classes and meetings. She joins our resident meeting to tell us it is essential that we think about the future of the Ashram. She emphasizes reflection time again.

She says, "It is not enough to think you have done some reflection and tell yourself, 'Yes, I think I can make a commitment to the Divine.' No. That is not enough. That will not get you there. You must be willing to give your all.

"What does it really mean to be committed? Do not worry about what people think of you. Being a good teacher will not carry you. You have to have more than just a satisfying feeling that you have done something wonderful. In fact, if you have that feeling it may be coming from the ego and will be a barrier to keep you from the Divine."

I think about surrender: I have to learn surrender more and it is best to start with little things. I must put aside my self-will. It is possible to turn my self-will around and direct my will to what is asked.

I also reflect on what Swami Radha said recently about our impatience to have some results from our practices. I really relate to this. She said we think we have done so much and we wonder why we have not been given a sign, some kind of reward for our efforts. But we have no idea what our backlog of karma is, how much has to be balanced out. It is our own self-importance that demands some kind of a sign.

But I see another side: the lack of results may show that I am doing something incorrectly. It is not that I demand the Lord come to me; it is rather that I am somehow blocking the possibility of that experience without knowing what I am doing wrong. Or I may be too dense. And all I can do is to keep going, doing my best, never knowing whether I will ever have that experience of oneness. But there is no other choice. Just keep going. And be grateful for being here where I have more opportunity to serve and to make that connection than anywhere else.

July 31, 1988

On my birthday all I can think about is Mataji. She is desperately ill. We all chant the mantra for her in the next room. My heart aches for her and what she is going through. I feel so helpless. The only way I can help is to put her in the Light and chant for her.

I do take some time to reflect on my life and all that Mataji has done for me. I ask, "If I die tomorrow, will I have lived my life as an example of the teachings? What quality have I brought into my life? How much time do I waste?" Is it wasting time if I want to be quiet and not do anything? Why do I think that I always have to be accomplishing something concrete? Quiet reflection is not wasting time.

What have I left undone? I feel an urgency now, not knowing if Swami Radha will be with us much longer. I want her to know what my commitment is to her. So I write her a letter making a commitment to dedicate the rest of my life to her and her work. I think about *sanyas* as the next step. Is this what is left undone?

August 1, 1988

In the morning I am awakened early by a storm; long reverberating rolls of thunder; hail and rain; the wind stirring everything up; a total change in the atmosphere. It feels like Mother Nature's response to Mataji's grave illness.

After breakfast I begin to feel queasy. My stomach is upset; I try different medications but nothing helps.

Mataji sleeps in her room, but is all right. I want to attend the introduction to our first Hidden Language certification workshop[1] tonight, the beginning of our Teacher Training program, but I am too sick to make it. I stay in bed and sleep, feeling sad.

---

1 Yasodhara Ashram offers certification to teach the Hidden Language Hatha Yoga to people who have completed the Yoga Development Course.

August 4, 1988

Swami Radha's condition has gradually improved and I come to her room to check on her. She tells me she is very touched by my letter of commitment. She shows me an elegant cotton dress made in India with sequins all over it and hands it to me, saying I can wear it for something special. She smiles at my enthusiastic response. Then she surprises me by asking, "What piece of jewelry of mine would you like?" She feels she has little time left so she is giving away many things, and feels an urgency to complete projects.

"Oh, Mataji, you've given me so much. Why don't you just choose something for me." She selects a striking gold bar pin with three diamonds. "These diamonds were removed from a ring given to me by one of my students. The setting needed some work so I decided to have a pin made. If you look carefully the largest diamond has a minute chip out of it, the middle one has a slight yellow cast to it, and the smallest one is perfect. That can be a symbol of your life and the phases of your development."

I always thought of the three diamonds on my engagement ring as representing my three children. But these three diamonds are symbols of my development.

August 7, 1988

Swami Radha is getting her strength back and I have breakfast with her sometimes. This morning I talk with her about *sanyas*. I am still in conflict – part of me is ready and another part is balking. She says, "Just look at what would change in your life. Maybe you would find out that things would not be that different."

"I know, but I am still not sure about the family."

"Margaret, you will give up attachments, not the family. For instance, you can tell them if they want to see you to send you the airline ticket."

I am sure they would do that, but I think she feels this is a way of testing how much they really want to see me. When I mention wanting to keep my investments in case of illness or incapacitation in later years, she agrees that is wise.

August 19, 1988

The Hidden Language Teacher Training is going well and I have enjoyed the teaching, but I have been bringing pictures and myths that are not in the Hidden Language Hatha Yoga book and one of the swamis tells me it is not appropriate. My first reaction is one of surprise and disappointment. The book uses myths to encourage us to look deeper and I have done so using my collection of pictures and myths in class to expand on the material. The students seemed to appreciate this.

Then I begin to reflect. What am I being told? There is a danger of going too far afield when teaching. Is it my ego that is being defensive? The book is new and there is plenty in it. There is no need for my own material. Also one of the strengths of Swami Radha's approach is to allow the student to make his or her own discoveries. It takes awhile for me to recognize the issue of self-will expressed in my attitude.

What was my motivation for bringing in pictures and adding more myths? Does my enthusiasm cover an element of showing off? It is subtle. One thing I must remember: this is Swami Radha's method and we are just starting to introduce it to others. We must stay with what she wants and how she wants it taught. I need to really look at my self-will and ask if it is getting in the way.

To show I understand what I have been told, I drop the use of outside pictures. This is surrendering and it feels right. But as I work today I can see how this issue keeps surfacing in my thoughts. I realize how important it is to discriminate between self-expression/self-gratification, and a sincere desire to allow the essence of the teachings to work without my doing anything.

August 24, 1988

Swami Radha has had a setback and is frail again; her voice is weak. I give her a foot bath that seems to refresh her a little.

Suddenly she challenges me about introducing the pictures and myths in Hidden Language. "Don't mix other things into the teachings. That is just entertainment. If you entertain students they will never get a real grip on things. Something that is fascinating or interesting should make you suspicious. There must be precision." She is highly critical and says it is the artist in me trying to express itself.

I reassure her. "I do understand now about not using other pictures in class. When I thought about it I realized that all the tools we need are in the book. So nothing else is needed. I know you are right."

Her look softens and she suggests I prepare a slide presentation of the pictures to show some evening. Then she continues. "Reflect on your drawings that are in the Hidden Language book and keep your focus there instead of looking outward for other things. Reflect on each picture and make a personal contact with it; write about what comes through. Direct your creativity in this way." This will be like working with a dream symbol.

Then she says, "I would also like you to do a painting of baby Krishna."

This is exciting. Focusing all of my attention on making this a work of love for the Divine will help me make a connection with the Divine, will take me beyond self-expression to a deeper place.

She has given me three options to replace the direction that I had taken inappropriately. She knew how to bring out the right kind of expression in me and I am so grateful for her guidance.

September 26, 1988

Swami Radha meets with us after the residents' meeting. Apparently she has decided the Divine is keeping her alive because she has something more to do and she feels that she must finish the temple. The foundation was laid in 1965, but there were so many other things the Ashram needed that the temple was never built. Now it seems urgent. She gives us lots of new ideas to get things moving – such as putting the word out to the Ashram community and friends. This is quite a surprise, as we have been focusing on plans to build a new kitchen and dining room. We will have to raise funds and do a lot of planning to build the temple.

It is hard to see her weak and in pain. How does she carry on as she does with her ideas for the temple, coming to meetings and keeping us all on our toes? Why does she have to suffer after all she has done and given to us?

Later Mataji calls me on the intercom saying I am a bad girl.

I am stunned. "What did I do?"

"It was what you didn't do! You forgot to make me chocolate chip cookies. Now you can't play in my sandbox."

Relieved, I ask, "Can I play in your sandbox if I bring you a chocolate chip cookie?"

"Well, I'll think about it."

I laugh as I respond to her playfulness and rush to bake her some cookies. She keeps her sense of humour even when not feeling well. When she comes out later to the kitchen she brings me a surprise. "Krishna's chocolates for you," she says, handing me some in a box. She thinks of others even in the midst of her suffering.

October 3, 1988

Swami Radha is much worse. Mitchell, who was with her last night, got practically no sleep, as she was up and down all night long. She is really weak. I stay with her so he can shower and we arrange for three of us to take turns being with her, and we set up a twenty-four-hour chanting schedule for the Ashram residents to support her.

I focus on the Light mantra or *Hari Om* while I am sitting with her. She sleeps for a bit, but when she wakes we call the doctor, who is very obliging and comes over immediately to see her.

The doctor takes blood samples and encourages Swami Radha to go to the hospital for more tests. I take the samples to the hospital, catching the next ferry to Nelson. By the time I get back it is 9:30 p.m. While I have been away, Swami Radha has agreed to go to the hospital, and an ambulance has taken her.

After all the intensity of the day, my energy drops as if I have been going on overdrive. I clean up Swami Radha's room and get things in order for her return, whenever that will be.

October 7, 1988

I go to visit Swami Radha in the hospital. I am shocked to see her condition, although her face does have more colour. She is under sedation from a test but she opens her eyes a little and smiles weakly at me, saying my name. She has improved with intravenous treatment and a blood transfusion. Now she has to take medication to heal her stomach ulcer, which has been caused by the aspirin she takes to control her severe arthritis pain. She is weak but her mind is clear.

I am going to stay to help take care of her with two other residents. The nurses are very understanding and are allowing us to stay in the room day and night. They bring a couch so that those of us on the night shift can get some rest. Swami Radha sleeps well all night. I repeat *Hari Om* or the Divine Mother prayer and when I do some sewing for her I silently say a mantra with each stitch.

We decide to take a hotel room where we can have turns sleeping while we care for Swami Radha. She sleeps a lot. The doctor talks to her about treatments. She keeps saying she wants two more years to finish her work.

October 9, 1988

Tonight while I am sleeping on the couch in Swami Radha's room, I awake in the middle of the night. Everything is quiet. I get up to check on her just to make sure she is all right.

I tiptoe over to her bed and am surprised when I hear her say, "Here comes my guardian angel." I sit on the edge of her bed and we talk. She is much stronger and starts talking about a dream she had some time ago of a grey void and the figure of someone in pain asking her what will happen when she has gone and we no longer have contact with her?

"In the dream I replied, 'Just think of me and everything will be all right.' When I awoke I thought, 'How arrogant of me to say that!' But soon afterward I read in Sivananda's biography that a similar thing had occurred to him when a disciple asked the same thing. He replied, 'Just talk to my picture and everything will be all right.' So I think this can be done. But always remember to put the picture in the Light. I don't want people to get caught in the personality level."

Then she tells me, "You can help other women with their dependency problems with men using your experience. You have a duty to do that. You must be careful that you don't slip back into your old patterns in connection with the family."

I assure her, "Oh, my direction is clear and my purpose is firm. I never would want to go back to the old situation."

"It has nothing to do with going back. It is the danger of being drawn back emotionally into old ways of behaving or interacting."

"Yes, you're right, I can see that danger is there. I have to be very aware."

She is her old self again with the Light and sparkle in her eyes and the warmth in her voice.

I am full of gratitude for this time with her. The intimacy and the opportunity to be on call for her bring me very close to her. I wonder about my past life connections with her. Was there a time before when I took care of her? Or did I not take care of her when she needed it and now is an opportunity to make up for that? I wish I could bring back those memories.

October 20, 1988 Victoria

Swami Radha's strength returned enough that she was able to leave the hospital. She arranged to have a couple of the residents drive her to Victoria. I followed today and am so happy to arrive and see Mataji up and around! She obviously is in pain but she is smiling and talking clearly.

October 22, 1988

I am restless as I am having many thoughts about *sanyas* and a strong feeling that I have to make changes or nothing is going to happen. I need to focus on my identification with Durga, knowing she is a symbol of the strength I need to integrate. She has all the qualities of courage, endurance and vision, seeing what has to be done and doing it! Her calm assurance going into battle on her lion tells me not to get caught up in the emotions of others. However, reading about her makes me realize she is fierce and this is also what I need in my life. Swami Radha has said that I am too easy, too nice. Sometimes it is important to be fierce. The account of Durga approaching her enemy, the demon Mahasura and his troops, gives a sense of her power. Her laugh rings out through the universe and shakes the foundation of the world. Her enemies tremble in fear and start to retreat.

November 14, 1988 Yasodhara Ashram

This is a very special time. I have a mantra practice of four hours a day for forty days – I chant between 5:00 and 9:00 a.m., and then attend Hidden Language certification classes for teachers led by Dawn. Swami Radha has often mentioned doing an intense mantra practice for a certain period. She says you will learn about your mind and how it works. This is the time for me to do it.

Last night I called her in Victoria. She didn't say anything about my mantra practice, but when I mentioned that I am starting to give away clothes and am finding a great freedom in that, she said, "You see?" She also seemed pleased that I am doing the reflections on the pictures in the Hidden Language book and she commented on the importance of that coming from a part of me.

But today I slip down into a totally different place.

My chanting brings up many fears: fears of facing nothingness; thoughts of death. Suppose all the lovely things I have read about death are simply the fabrication of peoples' imagination? Suppose there is nothing. What if I was aware and knew there was nothing? It would be like existing in a void, knowing I am there – total aloneness, nothing for support, unbearable desolation, no contact with anyone or anything. I haven't experienced this feeling of desolation before. It is terrifying and there is no way out.

What can I do? Where are all the wonderful things I have heard about death? Where is the Light? Where are the beautiful images? Here there is nothing, no sensory input at all. And where is time? Is this all there is forever? How can I stand it?

Is this the demon I have to fight and overcome? Other thoughts emerge, my higher self pulling back and forcing me completely on my own. I have to find my own inner strength, my own God or Goddess within. I have to develop a faith that has only itself to stand on. I must build something for myself. If I just sit and wait and nothing comes, I won't be able to keep going.

It sounds like I have outgrown a concept and need to replace it. This creates a feeling of insecurity. But a part of me says, "No! Not true!" A strong relationship has developed with Durga since she came to me quite spontaneously in the middle of the night months ago. She is there for me.

November 20, 1988

The four hours of chanting that I am doing daily is still bringing up fears.

It is the ego that doesn't want to die or change. It is the "I" of the ego that is experiencing this kind of death. The intensity of the mantra practice has brought this to the surface. I think the Divine has thrown me out on my own. Has this pushed me toward *sanyas*? I recall the overwhelming sadness at Swami Radha's impending death when I felt I had left something undone and she was leaving before I had done it. There was a deep karmic feeling connected with that. I have to let go and turn to Durga, my rescuer. She has come to me before and she can cut through this darkness and fear. Call on her. She will come.

As I chant I feel I am creating a cathedral of sound. I am building something beautiful. I am aware of my breath. Does this contribute to building something higher? I stop chanting and feel the vibrations in my body. The sound does have an effect. I need to empty myself of all preconceived ideas in order to receive whatever the Most High will give to me.

ten | SANYAS

March 20, 1989 Yasodhara Ashram

I am following Swami Radhakrishnananda, walking behind her silently. The countryside is open and almost desertlike in its brown colouring, with a few trees here and there in the landscape. One of the residents passes by silently and gives Swami Radhakrishnananda some food on a plate. I nod to her as I walk past but say nothing. Later in the dream I ask Swami Radhakrishnananda about this and she says it is a daily happening.

The *Hari Om* prayer is with me as I wake.

A feeling of reverence. I am following in Swami Radhakrishnananda's footsteps as if becoming a swami is the next step for me. She took *sanyas* a couple of months ago. Seeing her working around the Ashram in her orange sari has been inspiring for me. She looks so elegant and at ease, even out shoveling snow. In the dream there is a sense of quiet acceptance and a feeling of humility.

The other resident represents the pull of the outer world; she is attached to her children and has carried the mother role into their adult life. This warns me that I must not get caught in that trap but rather pay homage to the *sanyasin* part of myself, bringing an offering of nourishment. Swami Radhakrishnananda has had the courage to move beyond the ties of conventional family life in order to become a servant of the Most High. And she, in turn, is being served. At this point in my life, I can serve either my family or the Divine. I have a choice. The dream shows me very clearly what I have chosen to do. However, this does not mean that I abandon my family. It means that my focus is on the Divine and I can use the mother aspect of myself to bring nourishment to the renunciate.

After my practice this morning I look across the lake and see the rays of the rising sun shining on the tops of the western mountains in a cloudless sky. The air is crystal clear. I realize it is Swami Radha's birthday, a day to reflect.

I think about the importance of the sun. I can't actually see the sun, the source of the light, as it is still behind me in the east hidden by trees. But I see its effect, the brilliant light on the tips of the mountains gradually spreading down, clearing away all the shadows and darkness. That is how spiritual practices are. I can't see the source that creates the change as the Light begins to touch my life, bringing inspiration to me in the high places and then gradually moving down into the dim or shadowy places in my daily life: my attitudes, my work, my interactions. It has its effect, making changes that allow the Light of understanding, of compassion, into previously unclear areas.

March 30, 1989

I talk to another *sanyasi* who has years of experience with it. She points out that my area of testing is with my son and two daughters. I need to communicate what my focus in life is now in an inspiring way so that they can understand better. I have to turn them over to the Divine and if I do that completely and mean it, then I will see a change. I think I have done this, as they are on their own and I no longer think I have to make things right for them.

Later I write to them, trying to explain that I am letting go of old aspects of myself as a mother. I am not giving up my love for them, my connection to them, but rather coming to them in a fresh and new way without the old patterns of mothering, controlling and interfering. It's difficult to put into words and, of course, words can lead to misinterpretation. I do have a good relationship with them. They are all leading their own lives, but I know they wish I didn't live so far away. I am not sure how they will feel about this step I am taking. Trying to explain what I am doing has been very hard for me.

Sanyas is a deepening of my commitment to the Divine, making that my main focus. That takes precedence. I bring the awareness of my connection to the Divine into everything I do. *Sanyas* is a commitment to my own spiritual growth and development, regardless of what happens outside myself. It doesn't raise me higher than anyone else. It just says this is my focus; this is the means to get me where I want to go.

When I think about taking the step to *sanyas,* I feel right about it. When I think about not taking it, I feel disappointed, as if I am missing an opportunity.

I have a voice that says, "Can't you get there by just making your life a personal offering?" Another voice says, "Ah, but the commitment is much deeper with *sanyas*. It is like Durga going into battle – no distractions, no laziness."

Sometimes I think I don't have it in me to be a swami. But I know I just have to do my best and offer it back. Even if it's not much, as long as it is the best I can do, I just have to say, "This is what I have right now." Mataji says taking *sanyas* doesn't necessarily get you there. I have to do the work. *Sanyas* intensifies my focus, reminding me always: this is what I want; I have given myself over to the Divine. I have taken a stand and become a warrior.

April 19, 1989

Swami Radha arrives back from Victoria tonight. I am astounded at how perky she is. She walks in bright and vital, no sign of pain. What a relief! She looks so lovely and what a joy to see her smiling. She gives me a couple of warm hugs and I see she is her old self again. What a privilege to be here, so close to her. I am sure she has ideas to turn things upside down. We shall see.

July 17, 1989

I have been working on a Wheel of Life[1] painting that Swami Radha has asked me to do. I am almost finished. It has been a wonderful focus, to work alone in my room, learning new ways to use materials and becoming deeply acquainted with the symbols. Perhaps because I keep the *Hari Om* mantra playing and focus on the details of the painting, this practice seems like a meditation.

When I first started this project, I didn't think I could do it, but it has unfolded gradually. I figured out the technical aspects, such as how to make an exact circle without a compass big enough for the size of the outer wheel. I am learning a lot about patience by working in acrylics and having to be extremely careful with the tiniest details. This is very different from the free approach I am used to in working with watercolours. Every part of this practice has meaning.

July 19, 1989

When I tell Mataji about finishing the painting, she looks at me over her coffee cup and asks, "What did you learn from doing this?"

I pause and then reply, "Well, I learned to have more confidence in myself. And I learned that I really can focus when I have the mantra playing as I work."

"Did you learn anything about the symbolism?"

"Yes. While painting the monster that holds the wheel I thought about what holds me in a rigid place. One thing that came up is my fear of failure, of making a mistake, of not being able to fulfill my potential. I saw where my pride often prevents me from letting go of old patterns. Also, I think my self-will and selfishness are parts of a monster that separates me from the Divine. Wanting my way often prevents me from discovering other ways of doing things. I broke through some of that by listening to what other people had to say."

---

1 The Wheel of Life is a Tibetan Buddhist image, depicting the cycles of cause and effect, birth and rebirth, as well as the bonds and liberations of life.

"Anything else?" She encourages me to go deeper. She is interested in my process and wants to know what I experienced.

"When I painted the creatures in the hell realm I remembered times in my life when I felt trapped in painful situations. But then I painted the ladder and I saw that there is a way out. I have to be willing to let go of outdated aspects of myself and have the courage to pull myself out of the mire I have created in my life. I remember you saying, 'You are responsible for your life.' So I have to get myself out of the old stuff.

"I remember painting the figures falling into the hell realm on the right-hand side and thinking how my ego can lead me into self-pity or judgement, sending me right down into the hell realm. But if I am able to catch it, I can climb up the ladder on the left-hand side to a higher place of understanding and acceptance."

"You know, Margaret, that Wheel of Life painting will have an effect on you, particularly if you keep reflecting on it. Then when you are having a problem it will come in to help you. You will be able to ask, 'Did I contribute to that mistake?' And then you can see if you did or if it is just your uncultivated imagination."

August 18, 1989

Mataji talks to me about *sanyas*, making sure I understand that this initiation is a commitment of myself to the Divine, and the guru is simply a witness. In mantra initiation, the guru passes on the power of the mantra to the disciple and the disciple has the responsibility to keep working with the mantra and intuit its meaning. After the mantra initiation I am responsible for my relationship with the guru as this bears on her future as well as mine. The mantra initiation links the guru and the disciple together for future lifetimes. In this sense the guru is the Divine. The *sanyas* initiation, on the other hand, is the disciple's alone. The initiator assists. She does not pass anything on to me.

She asks me if I have thought of a name. I ask her, "Do you know?"

She replies, "Durga?"

"Yes! How did you know? Actually, Durga appeared to me so she chose me. I feel that having her name will be a reminder of the power I have available to me."

"That is true. And remember Durga has no consort."

She tells me that in the beginning as a reminder of the commitment I have made, I should wear a sari as much as possible, but that it is all right to travel in regular clothes. Some people who don't feel at ease in a sari might have trouble driving in one. Even Indian women have car accidents because their saris get tangled in the foot pedals. I get the impression that she is saying I should use discrimination.

The initiation will be on September 8th. I feel a glowing kind of excitement inside – a feeling of everything falling into place. The timing is right.

August 20, 1989

Apparently Swami Radha has told everyone about my initiation so it is not a secret. One of the residents asks me about sanyas. She has been thinking of taking sanyas herself, but has fears and doubts about it. I tell her I did, too, and I had to look at them and deal with them. The conventional stubborn part of me did not want to change or take a chance. It wanted to keep its control over my life, to be able to do whatever it wanted. The other part of me had a very different feel to it. It knew on a deeper level. There is extra energy available now from releasing the part that was resisting and holding onto the old. Making the choice and surrendering to it gives me a greater freedom. Even simplifying my wardrobe brings a feeling of lightness.

September 7, 1989

This is a day of preparation for my initiation tomorrow – chanting, reflecting, reading scriptures, praying. And, yes, even sewing my sari slip, repeating the mantra with each stitch. Later I walk to the lake and climb up to the little cave where Swami Radha used to sit in the early days. I feel protected, as if I am in a little niche like a deity. I think of being Durga sitting here with legs crossed, looking out over the lake, listening within.

I hear the voice of the ego speaking up for the security of leaving things as they are, fearing the change that is so vital a part of spiritual birth; it means the death of the old:

Like the Tower of Babel
The many voices interfere with clarity.
One says, "You are alone." It is the voice of fear.
"Your leap into the unknown will mean a fall into the
    darkest depths."
It is the voice of doubt.
"You can't make it." It is the voice of despair.
Where do these voices come from?
The insecurities of personality aspects unwilling to move or
    change,
They clamour like mere chattering creatures of the Earth.

But another voice cuts through them like a shining sword. The Durga aspect within me counters:

"Of course, you are alone. You are born alone and will die
    alone.
And yet you are never alone. For I am with you always.
My flame will light your way.
My shield will protect you from the enemies within.
My sword will cut through all negativity
Separating the useless stuff from the treasure.
My arrow will fly straight and true to the goal. It shall not
    miss the mark.

My lotus will lift you up out of the murky waters of your
    mind
Into the Light of Divine inspiration.
My mount is your mount – the ever faithful, loyal lion of
    the sign of Leo.
Remember you are never alone with my presence radiating
    from your heart.
Always be open to my guidance.
I am with you."

Thank you, Durga, for your strength and clarity. Be with me always.
I am aware of you standing behind me in all your glory and radiance. You
show me the direction; you give me the power. You shine within my heart
as well. May I always be aware of your inner presence.

I think about my gratitude to Swami Radha for all she has done
for me – her guidance and encouragement. I have savoured these moments alone. My day has been a constant prayer as I have moved from
one practice to another, keeping the mantra with me.

My life will be a fresh dedication to the Divine, a new start. This
is an opportunity I must not miss, and I pray that I will be able to bring
all the qualities of devotion, dedication, joy and wisdom to the life I
will be leading and the work I will be doing.

September 8, 1989

I wake up to a clear sky, the early morning sun highlighting the tops of
the mountains. This does not last long as the clouds roll in, painting a
grey wash over the day. No matter, this is my initiation day and it will
be a Durga day. I spend most of the morning doing practices but as the
time draws closer to noon I go to iron my sari. It is a beautiful orange
silk sari that Swami Radha gave me and there are about seven yards
of material to iron. One of the residents offers to do it for me, so I go
to pay my respects to Swami Radha, but she is talking earnestly with
someone and I do not stay.

The ceremony takes place on the temple site where the bare un-finished walls rise toward the shifting clouds. Tools of all kinds and sizes have been pushed back to make an open space in the middle. Large sheets of plywood lean against the sides. It is an unusual setting but I like the openness with the sky as the roof.

Swami Padmananda is the witness for my initiation and four other swamis are here to support me. One of them plays the *Hari Om* mantra on the harmonium and another has offered to take pictures. I have difficulty lighting my candle as Durga makes her presence known, whipping up the wind as if to say, "I am here as well!" There is joy and lightness as we all laugh together. We persevere but finally a sprinkle of rain, although a good symbol for cleansing and new growth, raises the question: Should we stay here or should we move?

The weather today seems to express the forces that Durga represents. I look up at the clouds moving swiftly across the sky. I feel inspired and moved by the power rather than disappointed. I silently say to Durga, "Yes, I know you are here with me. I feel your presence." Suddenly the wind blows over a large piece of plywood with a crash. I take that as a sign that Durga answers me, but we must be practical. We decide to move to the prayer room in Many Mansions to finish the ceremony.

I pass around the *prasad,* a small piece of fruit for each person. Swami Radha's little dog, Sita, comes in to join us, sitting up and begging for a treat. How can I resist her expression almost like a smile?

We end with some chanting. Now I am Swami Durgananda Saraswati!

I go down to the lake alone and have a sip of the water, thinking of this small amount of water as a reminder of the nourishment available to me. I don't need to drink the whole lake to satisfy my thirst for the Divine. I only need a sip. I can come down at any time to renew my vows of commitment here at the water's edge.

September 9, 1989

I awake with the words in my mind, "Doing the Work, Holy Work." Yes, this is my focus and all work becomes holy work.

The silk sari will be saved for special occasions but I have another orange sari for everyday wear and it takes me ages to get it together. I feel very frustrated. The material is so slippery it is hard to handle. I am going to have to pre-pin the pleats so I can get dressed more easily. Once I am together I feel all right in the sari, actually quite graceful. There is a contrasting sense of humility combined with a feeling of standing tall and taking responsibility.

September 17, 1989

A most unusual baby. At first it is in the child's pose curled up in a ball. It has no clothes on and seems to be covered with baby oil, as its body is glistening. It goes into a series of advanced asanas, doing them with complete ease. I am amazed as I watch.

This must be my spiritual baby who knows the essence of Hatha without needing to be taught or shown; it is a new aspect connected to my initiation.

Swami Radha asks me if I have noticed any changes since taking *sanyas*. I tell her about the feeling of support I have experienced in my practice, the firmer sense of commitment, the joy, and the acceptance of wearing a sari every day, which has been much easier than I thought.

September 28, 1989

This is a special day, as we have a ceremony on the temple site to celebrate the completion of the raising of the eight main arches. They are huge and building them was a big undertaking, but they are up now and will offer great support to the temple and its dome. We all gather around Mataji amid the plywood and tools and unfinished walls. She talks about the temple as the Temple of Light, of the Light in all religions.

"Let us recognize the Divine in each other. If you do the Light Invocation, it should be quite easy to do this, because you can't say only you are in the Light. The other person is in the Light, too. Remember 'The Divine in me salutes the Divine in you,' with the palms of your hands together in front. How can you fight with people if you do that? In your reflection in the evening you have to remember where you have not recognized the Divine in the other person. Make an effort. It's your greatest reward when you can see that all people the world over – whatever their name, their colour, their race, their religion – have the Divine within.

"Here we want to be together in the Light. So the temple will be open as a Temple of Light, for those who want to find the Light in their own religion. Those of you who have been with me for a long time know I have never converted anybody, because it wouldn't make sense. My own Guru said to me, 'Don't think you have to make Hindus out of anybody. I am not even a Hindu myself. Take what they have. Make the Catholic a better Catholic, the Jew a better Jew, and so on. Take the material that is there.' So, the Divine in me salutes the Divine in you."

And she ends by bringing her hands together at her heart in the *namaste* gesture. There is something very powerful about hearing her speak about the Light in the middle of all the construction. It permeates everything even when things are unfinished and in a mess.

eleven | EMBRACING DURGA

October 11, 1989 Yasodhara Ashram

Swami Radha comes over to the dining room in Main House after supper to give a talk to the residents. What a gift we are given. The tables are all moved together and we gather around. In her talk Swami Radha asks us one of the big questions in the teachings.

"What is the purpose of life? If your wife or your husband or your children were killed in a plane crash, does that mean the end of your life? Can others be the only purpose of life? No. We are too small, too insignificant to fulfill the life of another person. It's all an illusion that we think we can. We don't learn from our pain." My thoughts go to how easy it is to become attached to spouse, family and friends. I was too attached to my marriage. I might have ended up trying to gain meaning for my life through others. It just doesn't work. It has to come from within me.

"Think about Energy with a capital E," she says. "Yogis say you only have so many breaths in a lifetime. Don't waste them. I would like you all to think for a minute: Where do you as an individual take the Energy from to think even one thought? Do you know where you get the Energy from?"

I ask myself, How do I waste energy that must come from a higher source? I clutter my mind with useless worry about the future – much of it will not even happen. I allow my mind to dwell on issues in the past that are over and can only be dissolved in chanting the mantra or using the Divine Light Invocation. It doesn't mean I shouldn't reflect, but I mustn't allow the issues to circle around and around in my mind, going nowhere. That wastes energy. I often waste time during the day in talk that is unnecessary, just trying to be friendly, talking about superficial things. When I am sick, talking makes me feel drained and I just want to sleep.

"You can have more energy available to you if you don't think about yourself and how tired you are. Just think of doing Divine Mother's work and letting her do the work through you and she will supply what you need.

"How much energy have you used? You have already taken a large portion from the source of Energy. Do you have any idea how much energy is left? How many thoughts pass through your mind during the day? How many days? How many weeks? Months? Years? How much of that energy is already scattered?"

I assume I feel tired because I have been working so hard. I don't take into account that my thoughts use energy even when they aren't expressed. Forming thoughts is a prelude to expressing them, and to put my thoughts together I have to use energy from somewhere.

It has never occurred to me that I might have only a certain amount of energy from a higher source available and that means I am responsible for how I use it. I cannot depend on some kind, generous, ever giving source to supply my needs without me doing my part.

"If you do not have any inkling where you use that energy, how you use it or where it comes from, what right do you have to just scatter that energy all over the place, without taking responsibility for what you are doing and without assuring that there will still be a greater supply?"

All this makes me think about energy in a way I've never thought about it before. What is my responsibility here? I can generate more energy through spiritual practices. The Divine Light Invocation is a way of bringing the Light energy into my body, including my brain. Mantra chanting is a cleansing practice for me. Although I don't understand just what happens, I feel more alive after chanting. Certainly Hatha Yoga gives me more energy if I do even a short practice.

I am also aware of energy flowing in when I do reflections on my dreams. But in this case I am thinking and that uses energy. The flow of energy must have to do with the purpose of the reflections. If I just casually skim the surface I don't have the same results as when I go deeper. Then a meaning resonates inside, particularly in the heart. That must be the secret.

October 16, 1989

I am talking with Swami Radha when she quizzes me about something in such a way that my mind goes blank and I feel stupid again, as I did in school when the teacher put on pressure and it made me feel anxious and tense. She may be doing this now for a reason, to sharpen my mind, to test me, but I do find it difficult. I know her Tibetan guru[1] did this to break her concepts and it was shattering for her. I can understand that now, even though she is not firing questions at me the way he did at her. I decide to write up the incident to get clear about the emotions I was feeling, and I give her a copy.

October 19, 1989

Swami Radha calls me in and tells me she read my paper. Then she gives me such a boost I can hardly believe it.

"You are doing fine. You have very little work to do on yourself. Don't make a big deal of your minor shortcomings. Make a big deal of your connection to the Divine."

Then she gives me some ideas about how to bring vitality to my

1   Swami Radha met and visited a Tibetan guru in India. His teachings were a great influence on her own understanding of the Kundalini system. She writes about her experiences with him in *In the Company of the Wise* (Spokane, WA: timeless books, 1991).

practice, to my worship, such as illustrating my diary. She says it is fine to vary my practices and do the mantra in different ways, even walking around the room or taking it outside. She tells me to value what I have already accomplished: "Make a list of what you have learned from your years of experience as a mother and a wife. Focus on that and acknowledge the positive instead of getting caught up in the negative."

When I think about what I learned as a mother and wife, patience stands out, as I needed to be patient every day with the demands on me, the many crises, the household work, the children bickering or crying. But then I remember the rewards when we had sweet moments together, reading aloud or playing games and making discoveries in nature. I learned to not have expectations but to take each situation as it came. I could have allowed family members to make their own discoveries instead of expecting them to do things the way I thought they should be done. And I could have allowed my children to learn through making their own mistakes. I was not really doing selfless service in those years because I was into controlling things and wanted appreciation for my efforts. But I did accomplish a lot and I did care for my family. I think I need to accept my own mistakes as learning experiences.

December 5, 1989

I am staying at a place that I don't recognize in my waking life. I am involved with a young man and we are embracing when I suddenly realize that I have taken a vow and can no longer get drawn into emotional, intimate situations. I am a swami. I recall Mataji's words about celibacy – celibacy is not a moral issue; its purpose is to conserve energy for spiritual pursuits rather than the involvement in a sexual relationship. I am able to pull back before things get too involved.

A part of me seems to have that old desire to be wanted and loved, the familiar trap. It shows me how deep those old tapes go, the desire to be attractive to someone else, to be special. It is reassuring that I caught it, that I affirmed my vow, the power of the change that I have made, the acceptance of a different way of being, of *sanyas*.

I feel uncomfortable in the dream about the man being too familiar. But if he is my inner masculine, a young vital aspect, wanting to be close to me, then that is a different matter. It is important to integrate my positive masculine aspects, but I do not know this aspect. How do I discriminate?

Later, I focus on Mataji and my feelings of gratitude. I do some *Likhita Japa* for her and make her a little book of the things I am grateful for. When the residents all come together to chant in Many Mansions, right in the middle the phone rings. It is Swami Radha calling. It is as if we called her through our chanting! She has been in Spokane and we are glad to hear that she will be returning to the Ashram before Christmas.

Christmas Eve 1989

Tonight Swami Radha meets with the residents and gives us a very powerful talk. She says that each of us has to find the way to best make a connection to the Divine from the heart. Doing hours of mantra through sheer willpower will do no good if the feeling is not there. She had no one to guide her, so we should be able to find our own way as she did. If you worship Radha, you can make it in one lifetime. Radha stands for life and everything it embodies.

It is better to do reflection and work on dreams than to do mechanical mantra repetitions. She mentions the importance of checking out your interpretations of your dreams to make sure you are not fooling yourself. The mind is tricky. She once again emphasizes dreams as a spiritual practice.

She also talks about renouncing our need to be seen, to be heard, to be accepted. If we can do this, then we will become invisible – not like a "wallflower" where our insecurity creates a negative kind of state. No, it has to come from a decision of will, from a place of strength.

As I hear this I have a flash of a memory, standing along the wall in dancing class in those painful early teen years, waiting for a boy to ask me to dance. My insecurity was overwhelming and I hated being in this inferior role of depending on the opposite sex, the power given to them. But I now know how withdrawing the need to be heard and noticed and accepted gives more power to me on the inner level. I have tried this a few times at social gatherings. At first my mind is judgemental as it watches other people talking mindlessly or laughing too loudly. But I know a part of me does that as well. I don't like being in that judgemental part of my mind, so I have to change it by thinking of everyone in the Light. Just to observe, being in myself in a positive frame of mind offers great freedom. I don't put in my opinions but I answer questions when asked. I am accepting of myself as I am.

January 1, 1990

I am going through more of my things to give away. When I tell Mataji I am leaving certain things to Dawn in my will, she says, "Give them to her now." Of course, that makes sense. Then she tells me she has been impressed before with my quiet acceptance of renouncing things. I wonder what she is referring to.

January 7, 1990

A van of furniture is going to Spokane and I am sending the single captain's bed I bought after the breakup of my marriage. It is for Swami Radha to use when she visits there. The antique desk that belonged to my father is also going there for Dawn. As the bed is carried out the door, Mataji asks me, "Do you have any regrets about giving up the bed?"

Without any hesitation I reply, "None at all." I am amazed to hear myself saying, "It's good to have a change every so often." I must be learning from her.

"Now that your desk is gone you can have one of my desks. I would also like you to have my rosewood filing cabinet as you seem to need one."

I am touched by her generosity and respond that I would like her to have the carved dragon lamp that I bought in India. She is delighted and puts it on her desk in the living room where I can still see it and appreciate it. As I look at the lamp there, I am reminded of her telling me that when she gives her jewelry away, she then has the pleasure of seeing it on other people.

I am given one of the Ashram-built beds, which fits perfectly into the back corner of my room. The ease with which Swami Radha offers me her desk and special filing cabinet shows me she has no attachment to things. She has said people need to move around to different quarters so they don't get attached or too comfortable. I feel very fortunate to have been able to stay so long in Many Mansions.

February 14, 1990

Doing my mantra practice this morning, I close my eyes and see Durga, her arms opened to me. I go to her and feel her embrace me as if I were as a child. She enfolds me with two arms and I realize her other arms are faint shapes behind her, power that is potential. I need her soft embrace right now. I surrender to her and to the sound of the mantra spiraling around me, resonating in my heart. Mind has let go. It is still. I am just being here filled with awe and wonder. This is grace.

> Most precious One, I call to you.
> Please stay with me always.
> I feel the wonder of the child
> When I prostrate at your feet,
> Ego put into proper perspective
> By your big toe rising like a mountain
> Above me.
>
> Then I hear your playful laugh
> Coming from deep inside.
> And I ask,
> How can you be so small to fit inside me?
> Silly one, she seems to say.

If I am in your heart
Does that not mean
Your heart is big enough to hold me?

May 9, 1990

I am in a house that resembles the house of my childhood. Mataji is there, carrying a baby on her shoulders. She bends over to show the baby its reflection in a mirror and they both laugh.

Mataji is carrying me on her shoulders, taking responsibility for me, a baby in my spiritual search. She helps me see myself by showing me what I look like through my reflections. Mataji carrying me also tells me I am carried by my higher self and by Divine Mother.

July 7, 1990 Victoria

I am visiting with Swami Radha in Victoria, and she invites me out with a couple of others for coffee and cake at one of her favourite spots. As we walk in I wonder what people think of my orange sari. I am still a bit self-conscious wearing it in public places. Also it is warmer than a skirt and blouse in the summer and I am always glad when there is air-conditioning.

Then we drive down by the water, as she has some places she wants to show me. We come to an area of sandy beaches and I see women in bikinis, children running around and playing in the sand, sailboats racing downwind in a brisk breeze. I suddenly feel a mind shift as I see myself back in the early days of family life, sitting on the beach in a bathing suit, diving into the ocean waves to cool off, rigging up my sailboat to take friends out for a sail. What would I have thought if someone had told me then that I would be a swami in a sari one day? That old life feels so incongruous and far removed from my present situation. And yet I have no feeling of being drawn back to those times. They were fun but certainly not sustaining or fulfilling. As the car drives past the beach scene I return to the present, feeling happy to be here.

July 22, 1990

Swami Radha has given me some books to read. When I finish reading *The Divine Player*[2], she asks me, "What did you get out of it? What did you understand?"

"Well, I think one thing is the importance of a spontaneous, joyous, free approach to the Divine. It is all right for me to become identified with the Divine through Radha or Krishna, even though they are only symbols of the Divine power, manifest and unmanifest. But then I need to create a place in my mind – an image of Goloka, Krishna's heaven – in order to connect with Radha and Krishna on the feeling level. Also I know that I have to go beyond name and form and always put the images I use in the Light. If I do that, then it is all right to use those symbols to connect to the power they represent."

She reminds me that I must be aware that there are different levels of emotions and it is important to distinguish the higher levels, as those are what I want to develop. I used to think of emotions as negative, coming from the emotional centre in the solar plexus, and feelings as positive, coming from the heart centre. But I know that an emotion like passion for the Divine is not the same as something like a passion for competitive sports that has too much ego invested in it. Emotions can fire me up to do something, to take action, but I don't want to get entangled in them. I think emotions are often self-centred, where feelings are of a higher nature and take in something more than my little self.

I tell her, "I want to use the images of Radha and Krishna, with the flavour of what Goloka represents, the colour, the dance, the joy, and the love for Krishna which is really love for the Divine. His image connects me to that love. This is how I can establish the feeling and connection. This is what works for me. It is a bridge to the Divine, because Radha and Krishna are the Divine in a form."

---

2 David R. Kinsley, *The Divine Player: A Study of Krsna Lila* (Delhi: Motilal Banarsidass, 1979).

"Yes. That is good," she says. "I am very pleased that you have read *God As Mother* and *The Divine Player*. I want to lend you my copies so you can mark what I highlighted. Then you will know what I found significant. You may learn something from this."

July 23, 1990

I spend most days going over the books Swami Radha has loaned me and making notes. She keeps expressing her delight with this. Being steeped in the inspiration of the ideas in these two books helps shift me out of the old role of thinking I have to be doing all the time. Instead I am quiet, reading and reflecting and taking in the feeling of the worship of the Divine as a joyous happening. The inspiration has had an uplifting effect on me.

Swami Radha says to me, "I am glad you are not caught up in the kitchen, back in your housewife role. You are spending your time profitably; and this will act like a magnet that will attract more to you."

I receive one important insight from reading this material. I used to see Radha and the *gopis,* who were married, as indulging in immoral activities with Krishna, running off to dance and have love trysts with him in the forest. Now I understand that he is the original Source or Loved One, so their marriages are the distractions that have taken them off track. Krishna's flute draws them back to their real and original love. This completely reverses the story and it makes much more sense. Then I remember that Swami Radha has often said that even in a marriage relationship, the Divine has to come first. It is important to look beneath the surface of myths.

She talks about how a job in the school district gave one of the women residents the necessary firmness to put her foot down when needed. I am surprised at how understanding she is of my not having that ability naturally because of my role as mediator in my marriage, smoothing things over in the family. But I know it is something I need to work on. She says, "It is not in your nature to be that way and I don't want to force you to be a way that is not natural to you.

I see you as the illustrator of my books." That really touches me; it is such an honour and a gift!

"But you need to take daily awareness one step further: Question everything you do – what does it mean? I am thirsty; I want a drink. What does it mean to want a drink? What is a drink? I am tired. I want a rest. What is a rest? Can I rest with my mind still going? How do I rest my mind?"

In one sense this kind of awareness would keep my mind going every minute, but I think she is showing me how to develop more awareness in the present moment.

When she said my main focus of work is illustration I wonder why I don't give it the importance that it is due. I need to think of my artwork as primary and fit other things around it with the understanding that I am the illustrator.

August 1, 1990 Yasodhara Ashram

I call Swami Radha after my return from Victoria. I am sad to hear she is in a lot of pain. She sounds fragile and far away. I have difficulty hearing her, but I try very hard to pick up her words, as they are so important.

"I have a soft spot in my heart for you, Durgananda."

I reply, "And I feel that way about you, Mataji. I feel so frustrated that I don't have any recall of our past connections. I just hope that maybe I will have a dream sometime."

"I think we came back this time together to help each other," she says. I am deeply touched by this thought, as helping her is my greatest wish.

December 29, 1990

Today is Dawn's *brahmacharya*[3] initiation day! She had a dream about

---

3 *Brahmacharya* is an initiation with an emphasis on controlling all outward-going energies, sense enjoyments and emotional reactions, to give full power to the development of the individual.

baby Krishna that gave her the message that this was her next step. Yasoda is baby Krishna's mother, so that is the name she chose.

The ceremony takes place tonight after supper. Seeing Dawn take this step, I feel it is very precious, our spiritual paths moving closer together. *Brahmacharya* has to do with purity, and what it means on all levels. Like the other initiations, it is very simple yet powerful. When it is over, the new Yasoda says, "I didn't know it was that easy; why didn't someone tell me?" We all laugh. I am so glad she is now Yasoda. *Brahmacharya* can be a step toward *sanyas* and involves a commitment to the Divine as well. It connects us together in a new way.

March 29, 1991 Victoria

I am happy to have the opportunity to be back in Victoria for another visit with Swami Radha. Tonight we have an Indian meal with wine. Before we start eating, Swami Radha lifts her glass. "I want to toast Durgananda and – how many years have we known each other?"

"Twenty-four."

"Has it been that long? Well, here's to the twenty-four years we have known each other. Also to the ten years you have been at the Ashram."

As we sip our wine she mentions our correspondence in the early years and how I kept in touch by sending her donations regularly. I remember that being important to me.

April 5, 1991

After I help Mataji with her exercises, she invites me to sit with her and talks to me in a gentle way. "I have always been able to depend on you, Durgananda. You have done what was asked. But at times I have to come down on you a little. I hope I haven't come down too hard." I respond, "No, I want to listen to what you have to say and it is good for me."

Then she talks about our connection to the Divine. "The Divine as a child is not threatening. As Krishna changes from baby to boy to youth it is not the Divine coming of age but we who are coming of age. Krishna's battle is what everyone has to carry out. You can't cater to convenience and comfort. If the guru doesn't do his or her job, then the guru and disciple both go to hell." This startles me and I see how it puts responsibility on both of us. I hope the effort I put in helps and that if I slip back, I don't lose everything I have gained.

Tonight she is working on the German translation of the Kundalini chakra mantras when I go in to say goodnight to her. Her focus and concentration is so intense she never heard or saw me come in. That is the kind of one-pointed concentration I want to have!

What I get from being with Swami Radha is a feeling of her intense dedication and commitment. There is a sense of urgency now, a feeling that there isn't much time. If there is not a core of really dedicated aspirants, her work, her teachings, will not be carried on. The attitude of people has to be addressed. A person is not expected to be completely dedicated before coming to the Ashram and may feel uncertainty. But once the decision is made to live there, that is a completely different matter. The attitude must be one of commitment. I see that this also means being willing to do more than is asked.

April 7, 1991

Before her morning massage session, I tell Mataji about my dream last night of an intense blue that didn't have any form.

She says, "It is important to recognize the Divine as formless. Look at all the images in this room. I use the images to remind me of where my focus needs to be. Even when I am talking with someone, no matter where I am, my eye will fall on Siva or Krishna or Divine Mother. This reminds me of the presence of the Divine, in a form but also formless.

"The practices are to sharpen the mind, improve concentration and memory. Study the image until you can reproduce it in every detail. It is not that the practice makes you holy, but that it makes the mind single-pointed. By focusing the mind you gain power that allows the mind to develop or expand to a larger concept. If your goal is to reach Liberation and you are single-pointed about achieving that goal, then you may start with a limited mind, but as you keep it single-pointed on the goal and do the practices, your mind becomes able to soar to new levels."

As she is speaking I remember doing an exercise from the Kundalini book, concentrating on a spectacular rose, just sitting there and looking at it, taking it all in, completely absorbed. But I could not paint it completely from memory.

"The Cosmic Energy is formless when it is unmanifest. It is symbolically represented as masculine. Think about it in biological terms, the male producing millions of sperm for creation, more than are ever needed. Then when the Cosmic Energy manifests, it has a form that is represented by the feminine. In biological terms, the female egg embraces a single sperm and unites with it, growing into a new life form. There is always more creative potential available than is actually manifested. Remember this is sometimes symbolized by showing the male god being larger than the female goddess. Most people don't understand this symbolism."

This makes so much sense. There are thousands of maple seeds on the trees in the spring, spiraling down to the ground on their little wings. Maybe only one takes root. It also tells me how important that single egg is compared to the hundreds of sperm. But both are part of the creative process. I have more potential than I can ever use. What an idea! I wish I had understood this earlier in my life. I didn't question the concepts I grew up with that undervalue the power of the feminine, yet my parents made sure my sister and I got a college education.

I reflect on Durga and I realize she has given me a wonderful sense of completeness in myself. She has the strength and the power that I need to carry things through. She is independent. She was born of Light. She is Divine Energy manifest. She is active. She has the tools and weapons necessary for battling my inner foes. She is the perfect combination of male and female for me at this point in my life. I can

146

now own my strengths on both sides. I have only to keep my focus on her and see how quiet and calm she is in her activity, in her work. She is the protector, the provider, the nurturer, the creator, the assertive part and the receptive part, the one who starts something and the one who finishes it. She is complete in herself. This is the gift she gives me at this time in my life. I am grateful that she has come to show me another way of being.

twelve | FAMILY RESOLUTIONS

June 9, 1991 Yasodhara Ashram

I talk with Mataji about my family's request that I go back East to attend my daughter Wendy's and Richard's wedding. She gives me a lot to think about.

"Are you prepared to defend your path, the Ashram, the teachings, if you are challenged? Can you stand up to strong questions? And what blessings can you give to your daughter? She has already made the choice to follow this path of development, so what can you offer? You have to think this through. Look at the various reasons she has chosen to get married.

"And do not tell people you have to discuss things with me. You have to take responsibility for your own decisions. It is best to say, 'I will think about it.' Then do so and write down your thoughts, the pros and cons. Then discuss it with me. You have to do your own thinking first.

"You have to test your convictions and not just accept what I say or do. You must find out what you think. You may have to rephrase things in your own way and get your own experience. But you cannot just say, 'This is what Swami Radha says.'"

This is very sobering. I can see I need to do some clarifying for myself.

"You can give your children a legacy by writing or taping your diary, your thoughts on making the transition from motherhood to becoming a *sanyasin*. This would be passing on your own wisdom."

This is something I can do right now. But I still want to clarify, so I say, "It is my understanding, Mataji, that I should check things out with you in my first two years as a *sanyasin* and get your guidance."

"Yes, but you still have to do what you think is right. You have to take responsibility."

I reply that I have always felt it was important to build my inner security from my own experience, one step at a time. This is where my inner knowing comes from. I don't feel I have to defend that, but I will do more reflections as she has suggested.

When I think about what I brought from my time as a mother to my experience of a *sanyasin*, the whole idea of surrender stands out. As a mother I had to make the family my focus, especially when the children were little. I was often so tired. I remember times when I heard the baby crying and I went in to comfort her and she kept crying. "What is the matter, why is she still crying?" I was dreaming, that was the matter!

I learned to surrender to the needs of the family in the moment, especially when a flu bug went from one child to another. It meant being there and giving all that I could. Listening: yes, the importance of listening, not only for their calls in the night, but also to what the tone of their voices said beyond the words. In the early years the importance of control had to gradually be renounced as they got older and needed to have their independence. I learned how to show care and compassion, and know when to hug and when to be firm.

When I became a *sanyasin*, surrender, listening, care and compassion, giving up control, and being firm all came into play in different ways. Being a mother and being a swami go hand in hand except the swami opens up to a larger family, those who are in need, and the commitment is to the Divine. I think about my own spiritual baby that needs love and attention to help it flower into a wise spiritual being.

July 22, 1991

This summer we are celebrating Swami Radha's eightieth year (although her real birth date is in March) and this afternoon there is a tea at Many Mansions. Everyone is chattering away and the video camera is catching the action. Swami Radha sits in the shade under the laburnum tree by the fishpond where the birthday offerings are presented to her. We gather to watch her open the gift of the baby Krishna doll. A local doll-maker created the doll based on our instructions and a picture of baby Krishna. We wanted the little fellow to resemble the image Swami Radha had in a special dream that she often mentions.

When she opens the box and peers inside, her face lights up, radiating joy and Light. She laughs with delight and lifts the little fellow up for everyone to see. Then she holds him in front of her and looks into his face. "I can't get over it, he looks just like the baby Krishna in my dream!"

She tells us later, "I thought this celebration was to put the Ashram on the map, but I realize that it was actually for me." I am so glad she understands that.

After this excitement we have supper on the beach and launch the *Likhita Japa* boats that everyone made earlier in the day. They are made out of paper with mantra written on them. We watch as they float away, the light from their candles bobbing up and down on the gentle waves, carrying the mantra out onto the lake. It is very peaceful and quiet as dusk falls, and gradually we turn to go up the steps and back to our rooms.

July 24, 1991

Swami Radha really challenges me again when I tell her I am going to the wedding. She fires questions at me, playing devil's advocate to make me think about how I actually feel about the whole situation. I listen to what she has to say so I can understand her perspective. I don't necessarily agree with everything she says. It is painful for me to hear her say that if I had done this in Sivananda's Ashram, he would have been very cool to me. I would have ended up on the periphery of his circle of close followers because it would have shown that I didn't really put the Divine first, that I was still attached to my family. I don't think I am attached. In a way I am quite separate from them now that I am living my own life here.

We also talk about finances and she clears up my doubts about having investments and still being a renunciate. As long as I am not using my income for myself it is okay. The interest from my money, which really isn't my money, is working for her and contributing to the work, so it is performing a valuable function.

Then she suggests that I move out of Many Mansions to an apartment in another building. Next she brings up the possibility of my moving to Victoria so I can work with her on a symbolism video and book. I realize I must be prepared to go wherever I am sent. I remember also that she often considers ideas that don't necessarily happen, so it is best just to wait and see.

July 30, 1991

I put the reflections I wrote about my trip back East on Swami Radha's desk before going to teach a workshop. The writing has clarified my perspective, and I feel the power in verbalizing my feelings. I see over and over how important Swami Radha's emphasis on reflection is and how writing it all down clarifies my thoughts, and that gives me a feeling of confidence and respect for my position. The power of seeing clearly seems to get the understanding right into my cells. Mataji never gave me the idea that I was going against my commitment if I had contact with my family, but she insisted on my being clear with myself.

In the paper, I address what Swami Radha said about not putting the Divine first. How can I not put the Divine first? The Divine is with me all the time. Durga is with me in my heart. She stands ready to help me, to support me. Her calm and peaceful countenance in the heat of battle gives me the message that I don't need to get drawn into emotional conflicts in daily life. How can the Divine not be first when my focus is with that aspect of myself? I remember Swami Radha saying that once you have learned to read you can't unlearn it. I feel that way about my new life. I can't undo it, because it is a part of me.

When I go back East I want to convey, through my actions and my speech, a knowing that helps my family understand where I am now. I am taking my commitment with me. I know this will be communicated through the power of my new name and my vows. I do not expect my family to pursue the goals I have set in my life, but perhaps I can inspire them a little by expressing my ideals, by just being who I am now. Here is an opportunity to put into practice what I have been taught. However, I have no attachment to any results. That is in Divine Mother's hands. I know where my heart is. I don't need to prove anything, because I can stand on what I have built for myself. I do not feel shaky inside, I feel strong. In that strength I can accept my family without any expectations for things to be a certain way. I can be clear in myself that the Divine will be my guiding Light.

This afternoon Mataji hands back my paper with a comment on the envelope: "Excellent. You can go. You are fine. Safe in the Divine net. I am assured." Wow! I can hardly believe it. I passed the test. This makes me realize that when Mataji challenges me, she does not necessarily expect me to do what she says; she may be challenging me to think clearly for myself. I had to think it through and know what I was doing, but I especially had to have the Divine connection.

Mataji tells me not to wear a sari to the wedding. She says there have been too many scandals in spiritual communities and I should not make the family feel uncomfortable. I make the statement of who I am through my actions and my speech, not through what I wear.

September 9, 1991

I go down to the lake. The flowers from yesterday's *puja*, which we scattered on the water this morning, are still floating. The two roses representing Swami Radha and her teacher, Swami Sivananda, have washed back to rest side by side against a rock near shore, just as those two dynamic people rested by the Ganges in their short time together on the Earth plane. They do not need to be in the physical body to be connected to one another. She has demonstrated her love for him through her complete surrender and dedication to the work, carrying out what he asked her to do. In every talk she gives she never fails to mention him and her gratitude to him.

September 15, 1991 Boston

Wendy's wedding day. I see my family in a new light. I take Ritchie's arm as he leads me up the aisle to my place. Carla, Wendy's maid of honour, follows, walking confidently, head held high. Then Wendy and Richard last, starting their new life together. I feel a sense that each of our lives has taken us where we are meant to be. The wedding ceremony is thoughtful and full of Light. The priest brings a lighthearted approach that puts everyone at ease. But he has some practical words to say that remind me of something Swami Radha might say. "The preparations are over, the plans are complete, everything is done; can you be quiet and still the mind now in the presence of God?" I can feel the change in the mood as stillness fills the church. He has reminded us of why we are here.

Later at the reception I have an experience that tells me how far I have come in my spiritual development when my former husband asks me to dance. We have a friendly relationship now, but I don't care to dance with him. However, in my old life I would have said yes just to keep things smooth. Now suddenly several personality aspects flash through my mind. Each one has its own answer that I can hear clearly. I don't want to come from any of them; I want to come from that new place. I hear myself politely saying no. It feels like a victory over my old self.

September 23, 1991

This is my last night in Boston. I have had a good time visiting with various members of my family and tonight Wendy and Richard take me out for a Chinese dinner. They ask me about the Ashram, what it is like living there, what it means to be a swami, and what the teachings are about. It is very touching for me to have a chance to explain some things that have been a mystery to them. Their sincere interest shows me the importance of being here with them to explain about my life as they begin their new life as well.

Reflecting on my visit, I realize I was able to be a part of this family gathering, being myself, and showing the integrity of the decisions I have made in my life, without forcing anything on them. I didn't wear a sari to the wedding but I did wear it a couple of other times, and was happy when my sister-in-law commented that it looked lovely.

Yes, it has been a very worthwhile trip and I am full of gratitude.

My children, my brother and his wife, my nieces and nephews are not my only family. I have a second family in the people who live at the Ashram. I think about the core group made up of people who have made a commitment for at least two years; but the majority has lived at the Ashram far longer than that. We form a close relationship by working and living together. This connection deepens through our gathering in the Temple to chant for the prayer list. I feel very fortunate and hold both my families in my heart.

thirteen | STANDING UP

January 2, 1992 Yasodhara Ashram

I have been experiencing difficulties in my interactions with one of the other Ashram residents, David. We are not communicating well. I keep trying to sort out what responsibility in this situation is mine and what is his. I must be sure that I am communicating clearly. There is a reason for this situation and I want to understand it. Today we have a meeting and I realize I need to take a stand. I feel strong afterward and this is something new for me. We end up in a lighter frame of mind.

I see how I give my power away when I feel threatened. I do not like to deal with my anger or anyone else's. I am often aware of resentment more than anger in me. But anger is certainly the underlying emotion. If I hang onto anger and resentment, there is no way for the finer feelings, like compassion and understanding, to come in. I see my resentment surfacing when someone responds in a way that is not my way or wants to do something that is not in accord with my belief system. If I make a judgement based on this and feel resentment, I am limiting my perspective and shutting the other person out. Besides, I have made a judgement based on my self-will and ego. I don't want to continue this pattern.

There was unexpressed anger and resentment in my marriage – so much not talked about or resolved. I have unexpressed anger of my own and I fear this in others. I became the mediator in my family when others were involved instead of encouraging them to communicate and work things out. I wanted peace at any price, which never worked. I was unwilling to communicate, unwilling to simply talk about my feelings without blame or expecting certain results. I want to do something different in this present situation and let all these unresolved feelings go.

I remember something Mataji said to me a couple of years ago. I got up early and was surprised to find her already up. She invited me to join her in the sunroom for coffee and we sat by the windows looking out at the view of mountains and lake. She mentioned a student of hers who had been on her mind lately – a difficult person with erratic behaviour.

"Most people get very annoyed at her and don't realize that the Divine may send you a difficult relationship or situation to challenge your growth. I certainly found it very hard being with the rough and tough boys in the early days of the Ashram, but I know now I had to learn to accept them. They were with me for a purpose and it was not just to help with the building of the Ashram. I had something to learn from that situation personally. If someone gets angry with you and says some sharp things, ask yourself why the Divine sent you that message through that person. What is there for you to learn from it?"

As I sat with her that morning, I thought about the importance of learning from what she said about other people and using those insights for myself. Now is the chance to really do it.

January 10, 1992

I decide to do a longer mantra practice to let go of any negative emotions that may still be with me. When I stop chanting I become aware of a lovely, delicate fragrance that I cannot describe. Earlier I was aware of the lingering scent of the Indian incense which has remained since I used it yesterday, but this haunting scent is overriding the other one. Is it a message from the Divine? Just keep going? The Divine is with me even if I am not aware. I have the image of levels of density and something very ethereal coming momentarily through. It then moves back into its finer place of being. It is like a day when there is a thick cloud cover and suddenly there is a small opening in the clouds and a ray of light from the sun breaks through for a few minutes, then the clouds come together again. Here, it is the scent of the Divine. What a joy! I hope I can carry that with me today.

January 13, 1992

David and I decide to meet in a different way, to chant together in the prayer room in Many Mansions. I find this very healing. Can we elevate our relationship? I feel a coming together in warmth and understanding and compassion. It is very satisfying. *Satsang* afterward takes me further. There is an inner softening.

January 23, 1992

Swami Radha is traveling again. She is in Vancouver looking for a house that could be a centre. I talk to her on the phone and she seems pleased with a dream and a painting of Krishna I have sent her. She says something about "the flower is unfolding." I take this in to treasure it, as I so often feel I am not making any progress.

July 17, 1992

Today is the beginning of the dedication ceremonies for the Temple of Light. More than a hundred people are attending. Some of the people who lived at the Ashram in the 1960s and '70s are here and many of the people Swami Radha has known over the years. In the evening, we all walk to the temple where one of the swamis lights the oil lamp from a special flame. Then we all carry lighted candles as we walk around the temple, weaving in and out of the temple's eight doors, chanting Om. This walk commemorates one of Swami Radha's early visions of the temple where she saw people doing this. More and more people just keep coming, joining in the weave.

After we chant for a while, Swami Radha appears wearing a glowing white sari and looking so radiant it brings tears to my eyes. I think she is moved by the significance of the temple opening. She leads us through a visualization of the Light, telling us to see it entering through the top of the head and settling in the heart. This is the state of perfection.

"When you have found a treasure you keep it safe. The opening of the temple gives everyone here a treasure. Take care of it. Don't lose it. And remember to put all images in the Light; go beyond image into the Light. Never forget that." We will remember this because her talk was so full of heart and to the point.

July 31, 1992

My sixty-eighth birthday. It is hard to believe I am what some people would call an old woman. I do not feel old. I have lots of energy and vitality. I am so grateful for a healthy body and for the heritage of my family. I see so many people wounded and twisted because of what happened in their childhood or what they came into this life with. I do not seem to have terrible, dark, hidden fears. I have only ordinary ups and downs as we all do.

I think about acceptance. So often I see in class the difficulty people have accepting themselves, especially the goodness. I, too, have that critical voice inside. But "accepting myself" must not be used as an excuse not to work on myself. I cannot say, "This is the way I am," and then not make the effort to grow and change. Acceptance must never become complacency.

It is important for me to keep gratitude alive and with me constantly, as I could be called from this Earth plane at any time. I want to keep simplifying what I have. Let go gradually. Prepare for my transition.

August 22, 1992

Swami Radha gives a farewell talk at *satsang* as she leaves for Spokane tomorrow. Her talk is inspiring, sobering, electrifying. She talks about the Temple of Light bringing Light and love into the heart, making it a Path of Light.

"You will say that you can't love everybody. I understand that, but you can try to understand where the other person comes from, particularly the one who gives you the biggest problems. By looking at this, you can open your heart to let the Light flow through. Put yourself in the Light to get rid of your hostilities, resentments, rejections. You have to open the door of your heart and kindle the flame of Light and love in your heart. You must be fierce as a dragon to protect that and not let anyone blow it out or damage it. You are the custodian of that Light in your heart and in your mind."

I have the image of Durga being fierce in guarding the Light in my heart. I am glad that I have her protection.

"The Path of Light is the Path of Liberation. It is a gift. Take care of the gift and sometimes make a little gift to others because you have lots."

I feel overcome with sadness that indeed it could be her final farewell to us in the temple. She looks so frail in spite of the fire and the Light that is present in her. I wonder if I will ever see her here again. Tears well up and I feel my heart connection with her as she pauses at the door before leaving, bringing her hands together in *namaste* and looking at us all with her penetrating gaze. I feel the sense of loss that I will experience on the Earth level when she goes, and yet on other levels I know I can be in touch with her.

September 3, 1992 Spokane

Tonight is the ceremony to present the lotus ring to Yasoda, who directs the American branch of Swami Radha's work in Spokane (The Association for the Development of Human Potential, or ADHP). It is a duplicate of the one for the president of the Ashram. I give a brief welcoming talk. Mataji gives a long talk on living on faith and how each step evolved until the Spokane centre came into existence. She is really encouraging about the importance of us making a commitment. What goes right inside me is, "You can make it in this lifetime!"

She talks about Yasoda, the new director, emphasizing her dedication and commitment. It is very sweet when she prostrates to Mataji at the end. She has come a long way since our early days at the Ashram. I feel very touched by the evening and seeing Mataji's trust in Yasoda.

September 8, 1992 Yasodhara Ashram

My third *sanyas* birthday, a day that goes by too quickly. I reflect on my three years as a swami and know that I am solid about my commitment.

I do some reflections out loud and put them on tape. This helps me to clarify what my life lessons are. One is patience that I learned in my marriage. Another is achieving a balance between speaking up/taking a stand and listening/surrendering. If I am confident and clear, then I can take a stand for myself when necessary. But I always need to listen more carefully. When insecurity surfaces, that is when I need to shift my focus to the Divine.

Born Margaret Harper Wessels in 1924. Here she is at age 5. "Part of my story is discovering now that there were signs all along the way that pointed to my future direction."

Margaret and her siblings, Betty and Arthur, 1927.
"At the Quaker school I began to understand the idea of inner Light, as we sat quietly once a week in the Meeting House. No images, no dogma, no ritual – just sitting quietly and listening within. As a small child, I had squirmed and longed for the meeting to end. But in this school I learned about ethics, quality, creativity."

Margaret's drawing of Yasodhara, done in 1940, found over 40 years later. "Suddenly I come to a picture of the wife of the Buddha, Yasodhara! I am stunned, but there it is written at the bottom of the page. Did a part of me know?"

A sketch Margaret made during a class trip to the Boston Museum of Fine Arts in 1943. "I paused in front of a strange little figure, Krishna, dancing on the head of a snake... I made a sketch, put it aside and then forgot about it. I wonder why these two pictures are the only ones I saved."

Margaret and her 3 children, left to right, Wendy, Ritchie and Carla 1952. "That deeper knowing part of myself was buried in a life filled with raising three children, doing volunteer work, furthering my education, teaching, and the many, many things that make up a woman's life."

Margaret and her husband George, 1969.
"I have decisions to make about my marriage. Should I stay in it and work on growing and learning through it, learning to be inwardly free no matter what the outer circumstances are?"

Margaret and her daughter, Wendy, 1972 in India. "This was a temple honoring the warrior goddess, Durga. I didn't know any more about her but she seemed to touch the hearts of the people in the village."

The Mary seen from Margaret's new apartment window, 1979 "My eyes are drawn to a statue of Mary in the garden... She looks so serene and I feel she is giving me a message of compassion, sending me her protection."

Margaret and Swami Radha, November 1980, Philadelphia.
Swami Radha: "I am very pleased about the progress you have made over the last two years, though there is still more to be done. But if you have done this much in two years, just think what you can do in the next two years."

Margaret at her mantra initiation, September 8, 1984.
"We look long and deeply into one another's eyes. It is as if we are communicating on a level beyond words. Yes, Mataji, I will take the initiation to my heart and keep my commitment to you clear and true."

Margaret and her niece, Dawn, in front of Many Mansions, 1985. "How fortunate I am to have a family member who is interested in the spiritual path."

THE WHEEL OF LIFE

Swami Durgananda's drawing of The Wheel of Life, 1989.
Swami Radha: "You know, Margaret, that Wheel of Life painting will have an effect on you, particularly if you keep reflecting on it."

Swami Durgananda and family, Spokane, 1993. From left to right: Ritchie, Wendy, Carla, Debbie, Richard, Swami Durgananda, Yasoda
"I am very fortunate that all of them have a very caring side that they express in different ways."

Margaret and Dawn, now Swami Durgananda and Swami Yasodananda, 2004. "The thread of Dawn's story weaving through my life culminated with her *sanyas* initiation on Easter Sunday 2004. She became Swami Yasodananda, and our connection grew even closer."

fourteen | COMING CLOSER

April 2, 1993 Yasodhara Ashram

"Durgananda, Swami Radha calling from Vancouver."

I run to the phone. "Hello, Mataji."

"Durgananda, I have some surprises. I want you to join me in Vancouver for a little while and then we will go to Spokane. What do you think of that?"

"It sounds great, Mataji. I will get my things together and make arrangements."

What an invitation! I hope I can serve her and really be aware; it is a wonderful opportunity.

April 7, 1993 Vancouver

I arrive in Vancouver by early afternoon. After I settle in, I come to her room and we talk about how things are going at the Ashram. Then she focuses in on me. "When you came to the Ashram, Durgananda, you had a tremendous need for self-expression. But I think it is important to give people time to change. I just waited and you gradually came through that – you came around." I am glad to hear her say that. It shows I did surrender and learn the lessons.

We talk about teaching and students who are resistant in class.

"Remember that students who are under the influence of the fragile ego, feeling hurt, wanting to be noticed, wanting to be heard and recognized, are really not ready to start Kundalini Yoga. It takes too much discipline. It is important where you put your power and how realistically you see things." This rings a bell, not only for students, but for me personally. And yet I have been doing Kundalini for a long time. It shows how deeply ingrained these patterns are.

April 10, 1993

Dream recall slips away as I awake with a sense of gratitude to be here with Swami Radha. I feel relaxed and much more rested, no longer under the pressure of too much to do. My work at the Ashram has been taken over by others. It is as if the waters close over the space I have left. What is my future? Just going along with whatever is asked, offering myself to Divine Mother and accepting her guidance, serving my Guru. If I can put myself aside and be an instrument of the Divine, then I will have done what I am meant to do. It is an opportunity to keep Swami Radha in the Light and to keep myself clear as a channel. May Durga be with me and guide me.

As I massage Mataji's feet this morning I feel a wave of love and caring. Gratitude to have this opportunity to serve her. Compassion for her at this stage of her life when she needs kindness and care. Our time together is easy and I feel happy being with her.

Later I ask Julie if she would like to take a walk. She is Swami Radha's main caregiver and needs to get out when she has a chance. I always have this image of her at the Ashram bursting out of the door at Many Mansions and running down the hill to the office to do some photocopying for Swami Radha, expressing freedom with every step. Now we take a brisk walk together, enjoying the fresh air, the scent of flowers rich from rain earlier in the day. We talk about how important it is to get out for exercise and fresh air, but we know that is not always possible.

April 17, 1993 Spokane

We have arrived in Spokane and Swami Radha is thrilled with the apartment that has been renovated for her in a lovely old house near the Radha Centre. It is spacious and light. She walks around, exclaiming over the improvements, looking in closets, smiling and running her hand over the smooth dark wood of the fireplace. Now she has her own space and it has the quality of the old-world elegance that she was used to in her early life.

Later a big load of heavy furniture is brought in. There is much grunting and talking and stopping to measure to make sure pieces will fit. We move things around and discuss and shift and turn. The whole time this is going on, Swami Radha sits at her desk totally immersed in a book on Arab women. She seems oblivious of the activity around her until someone has to ask where a certain piece of furniture is to go. In a spirit of selfless service, we move and shift and carry – no complaining, just doing it.

At one point the group takes a break and talks about Milarepa, the Tibetan yogi, whose practice was to build stone structures, tear them down and rebuild them somewhere else on his guru's instructions. Our practice is to constantly move furniture. One person calls it "furniture yoga" and says it eventually wears down all resistance. We laugh and someone else says, "It just doesn't matter anymore. I am ready to move anything anywhere."

When we are finished Swami Radha suggests we order in food for supper as her treat for us. We eat on the porch, sitting across from her. She looks at us and says, "What a nice gallery of beautiful people. I have what no one can buy – real *gopis* and *gopas*."

As we pass around the food she talks about selfless service. "Back in the early days of the Ashram one of the young men slammed the car door on my fingers by mistake. It was quite painful but I held my hand up and said to the Divine, 'I need my hand to do selfless service for you.' And gradually the swelling and redness and pain disappeared and it was healed. So selfless service is very important."

Her words take me back to doing the Cow Face pose this morning, thinking about how the cow gives and goes on giving. I see how Swami Radha brings another dimension to this. She gives and gives even when she doesn't feel well. And her giving is not offering sympathy to people with their problems. Her giving may be to really challenge them in the hardest way. It is not easy for her and it is not what the other person wants, but it is what is needed for the next step to take place. I am aware also that she doesn't talk about her giving. This is something I need to look at, where I talk about all that I do. That takes away from the selfless aspect of the work.

She turns to one of the new aspirants in the group. "I want you to help with the upcoming books," she tells her, smiling encouragingly. "You see, if you have trouble with meditation, there are lots of other ways to use your talents to serve the Divine. And I do not believe in making people do the opposite of what they really want to do. If someone has a talent and an interest, then use it!"

"Now I want all of you to remember you need to live a balanced life. Take time to work outside and take walks. Don't get caught up in just working at your desk."

As our time together closes she tells us about some of her dreams and visions. Her voice becomes soft and the tone changes. "A part of me tended to discount them or say they were just my imagination working overtime. But then I would have a confirmation, usually through a piece of jewelry someone would give me that told me the experience was real. Pay attention to the messages the Divine gives or you may not receive any more." I notice her lip trembling and tears in her eyes. She must have touched a tender place inside.

April 21, 1993

I help Mataji in her bath. The tub is a large old-fashioned one and she can really stretch out in it. She enjoys it so much that I feel happy she can have this simple pleasure in her life. She keeps saying, "This is great!" She also exclaims over the way I can lift her up, but I tell her it is easy because her legs are so much stronger.

I really appreciate Swami Radha's spontaneous talks to us and am glad she joins us for supper tonight. It is so amazing how she just comes up with a subject and tells stories and pinpoints aspects of the Teachings. I always feel inspired afterward. Tonight she talks about gratitude and being receptive to the Divine. "You can't make something happen but you can be open and ready. The TV is no good without a receiver; the signal can't come through. You can't talk to someone on the telephone if you don't have a telephone at your end."

This is something that has been concerning me, as I need to still my mind in order to connect with her on that level and also make myself available to the Divine.

She also talks about sound and vibration. "The pyramids were built through sound vibration. In language there is meaning in the sound of letters being pronounced. In Hebrew each letter has a vibration or series of vibrations that is very significant. But in English we don't always pronounce every letter, such as the 'e' in James. So English doesn't have the same levels of meaning.

"Think about the power of a prayer wheel. That is vibration, too. You write the mantra thousands of times and put it inside the prayer wheel. Then as you turn the wheel you are putting something into motion – a great power. Of course, you can do that through chanting as well."

She also mentions building the beach prayer room at the Ashram in the early days. "One of the young men cut down young, green saplings to support it. You can still see them in the ceiling. Each night I would clear away the tools, put blankets down on the floor, as there was no carpet, and we would have *satsang*. Eventually we bought a carpet. It cost sixty dollars – I remember that!" She laughs. "Then I brought in some plants and the young man said, 'Now I guess you will have a greenhouse in here, too.' He always thought I had too many plants." Her laughter is contagious and we all join in, happy to hear her talk about the early days.

April 28, 1993

After supper we have a video session about dreams. Swami Radha has asked us to write down questions that she can use to talk about. I am filming her the entire time, so I give my questions to a Radha Centre resident. Swami Radha is in rare form and I find it quite intense. After an hour of taping we sit at the table and she continues with some powerful stuff on initiation and being Divine Mother's handmaiden. One thing that really hits home with me is about initiation. "There is nobody who has had an initiation who has really followed through on it – really investigated what it truly means. They say they are doing certain work or a project because they want to be someone special. But if they have had an initiation they are already special. They just don't accept it. They don't think about it."

I feel sad to think that I may not have followed through on my initiation. I have made a commitment and I want to follow through.

She continues, "You mustn't let rigid concepts and emotions from the past determine who you are now. But you have to use and accept what is helpful from it. You have to give yourself to the Divine, past and all. Radha has to accept my Sylvia nature or she isn't complete. And Sylvia has to accept Radha. You have to accept your past and build on it.

"Be clear that you are Divine Mother's handmaiden. Then you don't need acceptance; you don't need approval from anybody else. In the beginning, I got so much criticism from the seven young men who started out with me at the Ashram, I just thought I would pack up and leave. But then I thought, 'No, I'm not going to let them have that power over me. It doesn't matter what they think. What matters is that Divine Mother accepts me.'"

Yes, I know how easy it is to give my power away. The image of Durga helps me. With her power, she reminds me to own the power that is mine.

May 8, 1993

At the supper table the subject of women arises. Swami Radha talks directly about how they don't understand the use of energy.

"Often women misuse the neutral Energy which is Divine Mother. I remember once I was traveling with one of the young men. We were looking for a place to have supper. We ended up in a dining room that seemed fine, but then a floorshow started before we finished eating. A woman came out to dance with very little on, tassels and sequins and not much else. I watched the young man and his eyes were just about popping out."

She laughs with a sparkle in her eyes as she continues. "I leaned over to him and whispered, 'Can you see Divine Mother in her?' Because this was Divine Mother's manifestation used in a purely sexual way. Men see sex as a pleasurable thing and women envy a woman like that dancer because she is accepted by men. But men accept her only as a sex object, not as a truly human being. This is *maya,* or illusion, and you have to reflect on what this means. It is not enough to brush this off and say you aren't interested in it; you have to reflect on the meaning so that you are clear about it and have an understanding."

May 15, 1993

Swami Radha is so practical. I really admire this quality in her as she accepts the importance of living each day with responsibility. Today she talks to me about money and mentions a resident who, she says, needs to think more practically about it.

"She says she dislikes money. She does not want to acquire any. So I asked her, 'Well, what would happen if you had a dental bill of several thousand dollars; how would you pay it?' She said, 'I guess I would borrow the money.'

"So I said, 'Oh, you would go to someone who worked to save up some of this stuff you think is awful and take it from them to pay your bills! You better think about that.' Lots of people have that attitude and they don't think deeply enough about what it means."

I agree with her. My father was very practical and he brought the lesson home to me in many different ways. He wanted me to understand the value of earning money and putting aside some for the future, so when we were young he often offered to pay my brother and sister and me to do certain extra jobs around the house and garden. I remember picking Japanese beetles off the rosebushes and putting them in a jar. There were no pesticides in those days and there were a lot of bugs and beetles. We were paid so much per jar. I saved that money in a little bank I had in my room.

May 18, 1993

I decided to hold my *mala* last night. I repeated a mantra and went to sleep very quickly. Later in the night I heard a song called *Ananda Kutir*. It is a lively song about Sivananda's little house on his ashram in India. I awake this morning with the song still there. Is this because there are four pictures of Sivananda hanging right next to my bed? He seems to be with me.

Swami Radha has made a series of videos on various subjects for the residents to watch and then write about. She goes over some of my papers, starting with the one I wrote about the video on how she received a skull *mala*. It is quite a story that ends with a woman Swami Radha didn't even know giving her a *mala* made of little skulls. This woman felt uncomfortable about it and never used it. But after talking to Swami Radha she said, "I want you to have it. I feel it belongs to you." I have seen it and it looks very powerful, but it seems strange to have skulls instead of beads.

Swami Radha says to me, "You haven't gone far enough with how you can use what you learned from this. Don't just write about what I said. I want to know what it means to you. And whenever you discover any parallels in your life, acknowledge them. Then think about them and make use of them. What does the skull *mala* mean to you?"

I pause to think about it. "It brings up an awareness of death.

I remember reading about death being behind me, just over my left shoulder. That makes me think about death being present."

"What thoughts do you have about death? Do you mean the death of people close to you?"

"No, it is more than that; it is also the deaths I have experienced in myself. The death of concepts or parts of myself as I have changed or grown. They have all ended up being positive and making me stronger, so death in that sense has been a positive thing. I can use that when I think about my physical death."

"Durgananda, you should entertain some thoughts about that. Once I had a dream in which one of my students asked me about death. He kept pressuring me about how I would want to die, by fire or steel or water. Finally, I said to him, 'It doesn't matter how I die because I will be singing among the stars.'

"The unconscious will provide the understanding. I dreamed of the chariot that would come to take me home and there were no horses, but I knew the horses would be there when the time was right. This gives a certain ease to the idea of death. There may not be a tangible, sensuous heaven of Krishna, so what do we mean by heaven? Maybe the best thing is to think of singing among the stars.

"As you approach the end of the physical, think of yourself as that vortex of Energy that is your consciousness, and think about whatever your approach is to the Divine."

I express my main concern. "The only thing that would be difficult is if I were incapacitated in some way."

"Yes, that is true. But you can take the attitude, 'I have paid off all my karma, so now I can be reborn as Divine Mother's handmaiden, spotlessly clean, white, nothing attached.' Pray to remember who you are and what is your purpose."

This would take constant awareness. "That is why I try to keep the Divine Mother prayer with me going to sleep. I am sometimes aware of it in the night."

"That is good." Then she looks at me intently. "Durgananda,

do you realize how different your papers are now compared to when you first started? How they have improved?" I feel encouraged by her words, because I feel that in my papers I no longer just stop at one idea but consider different possibilities and different levels. I don't intellectualize my insights as much, and I work hard to make them real in my life.

May 25, 1993

My three children and their spouses arrive for a visit, the first time I have seen them since Wendy's and Richard's wedding two years ago. I am excited about being with them, but have to balance my time between them and Swami Radha.

She wants to be sure I have plenty of time with them so we go through her exercises and massage early. Then she gives me some money to pay for lunch at a restaurant. "You want to look nice when you go out to lunch," she tells me and gives me a beautiful dressy sweater of hers. I am touched by her kindness. I have a great time with the family, taking them to an elegant restaurant. At first I feel reluctant about spending Swami Radha's money, but letting go of that is also a part of renunciation. It doesn't seem like renunciation!

After our lunch we take a walk and then go back to the bed and breakfast where they are staying. My mind has been full of the talk about death I had with Swami Radha last week and I feel that this is a good time to discuss some of the issues around aging with them. I am very fortunate that all of them have a very caring side that they express in different ways. My son Ritchie and his wife Debbie are both very practical and have good, intuitive business sense. Carla has different kinds of experience from her artistic work in films and a sensitive side that I connect with. Wendy takes on responsibility and tends to worry, feeling concerned about my future. Her husband Richard has not had much contact with me since the wedding but he fits right in with the family and is very open. We all have a sense of humour that lightens up our gatherings.

Ritchie asks me if I have thought about what would happen if my health gets so that I can't live at the Ashram. Will I be staying here in Spokane? Of course, I don't know what the future holds; so much depends on Swami Radha right now. I am feeling very well and am glad to be helping with her care. But I can't expect the Ashram to take care of me if I am bedridden at some point. I would have to make other arrangements.

We all talk about what these other arrangements might be, like investigating options in Victoria or here in Spokane. I have written out a list of my health history, my doctor, and other information they might need, including my will and a living will. I want to remain independent as long as I am able. They suggest I pass on any ideas to the Ashram to keep them informed.

They know that I am taking care of my physical needs through proper diet, my Hatha practice and the amount of walking I do. I tell them I keep my mind alert by teaching and writing. And of course, doing my spiritual practices is vital for the spiritual level. I feel relieved that we have clarified some of these matters and am grateful that we can be honest and clear with each other.

June 11, 1993 Yasodhara Ashram

Swami Radha, Julie and I returned to the Ashram yesterday. Mataji has a lot of moving plans for the residents. Mary Ann will move into Many Mansions, as Mataji is training her to take on the leadership of the Ashram and wants to have her close by. She will be available for Mataji's care at night, and will work in the office during the day to get an understanding of how the Ashram functions. It seems like a demanding schedule but Mary Ann tells me that she will take one day at a time and not look ahead.

Mataji tells me I can keep the downstairs room at Many Mansions, which I moved into in February, but when I am not at the Ashram, others will be using it.

I am trying to get enough rest so I can be fresh and clear for

Mataji. I am surrendering to her and what she needs. Actually, I am surrendering to the Divine will, as that is my purpose. The less I resist or think about the way I would like things to be, the more energy I have. Mataji commented on this last night when I did her treatment later in the evening and did not feel tired at all.

After supper Mataji says to me, "So *satsang* is from eight o'clock to nine." She is wondering whether there will be time for me to help with her bath before I go.

I say, "I don't have to go to *satsang*. I'll do whatever is best for you." She looks at me quite intently and asks, "What is the difference?"

I think she is asking me what the difference is between attending *satsang* and helping her with her bath, but I am not quite sure. "I can go to *satsang* and help you with your bath at nine o'clock," I suggest.

"Durgananda, with the kind of commitment you have, there is no difference."

So serving the guru is the same as going to *satsang*. It is a form of *sadhana*, a practice. But I know it has to be done as an offering, not in haste or with resentment or any of those reactions. I have to be totally there and bring the best of myself to what I do. I tell her I will do whatever is best for her.

Later she tells me, "You are an obedient disciple. And remember that you are Divine Mother's handmaiden." To me that means making things as easy for her as possible at this time in her life, and she seems pleased with what I am doing.

June 18, 1993

This morning Mataji is flying high. She is up and down the stairs, full of energy, meeting with people, going from one thing to another. It is incredible. I hope she doesn't burn out.

I have been cataloguing books for her and also trying to get things cleaned up in my room. More things keep getting added to my list and now I am further behind than ever.

One of the jobs she has turned over to me is her filing. I feel at sea because I don't know her system. She keeps adding work and new areas of responsibility and I see where I am now doing the very thing I was avoiding in the past – being given too much responsibility. Then I was afraid I couldn't handle it; now I just do it and don't think about whether I can handle it, or whether I will do it right. I think she may be doing this to challenge me. I have to take responsibility and set priorities. I know I am functioning under her blessing, so just surrender! All that I am doing now is connected with my Guru and it is a privilege and an offering. Make it truly that and shift my focus away from myself.

She comes in while I am working and sits down with a cup of tea. I am going over the files, sorting through them, arranging them and removing some. I find a file on "Spiritual Commitment," personal commitments various people have written to her. I show it to her and she begins to read it. Then she sits staring off into space for a long time, as if she is somewhere else. Finally she comes back and says she wants to keep that file to read.

Suddenly she turns to me and says, "I can't understand why your husband didn't want you to stay in the marriage. You are so considerate and kind and easy to live with. Why would he want to give that up?"

"I think I have changed. When I was with him I was often upset but covering it up, and then it came out in outbursts and arguments. I think I challenged him in some ways, and he didn't understand my spiritual calling."

"Well, I find you are nice to have around. And I know that sometimes I am difficult to live with. I can be crabby and impatient."

"But you have a lot of things on your mind. Besides, you are always thinking of other people. It amazes me how you constantly give, even when you aren't feeling well."

She reaches out to me, smiling warmly. "Give me a hug," she says. Then she goes to her dresser and takes out a lovely orange prayer shawl. She hands it to me with a twinkle in her eyes. It is raw silk and larger than the ones I have had before. It is light yet has substance and it folds easily around me. I am delighted to have it and thank her for her thoughtfulness.

Tonight we have a Rose Ceremony and it is perfect for using my new shawl for the first time. During the chanting I think of the vibrations of the mantra coming into my new prayer shawl and permeating it with *Hari Om*. I feel like I am wrapped in mantra and I make this my focus during the ceremony. I send *Hari Om* to each participant who is putting the petals of the rose in the bowl of water. When I return to my room after the ceremony I write Mataji a little note of thanks to leave on her desk tomorrow.

June 27, 1993

Early this morning in my sleep I become aware of the subtle perfume of Mataji. It actually becomes quite strong and comes in waves. I wake up and lie there quietly wondering if I have dreamt it. But it comes back several times in an almost tangible way. I can't explain it rationally.

Tonight Mataji asks me to give her a foot massage. I feel such warmth for her when I do this and it is a way for me to give back to her. It has developed into an intimate time, just the two of us, me kneeling at her feet. We often don't talk and I put my attention on keeping the Light present. Sometimes she has her eyes closed, sometimes she watches me and when I look up at her she gives me a gentle smile.

This time she asks me what I am thinking.

"I was trying to keep with the Light, but then I found my mind was wandering. I was pondering doing one thing, like ironing or doing dishes, while thinking about something else. Would that mean I was doing it mechanically and not giving it my attention?"

"You know, there is a difference between giving something attention and concentrating on it. It is fine to think about something else while doing the other thing, but not all the time. It shouldn't become a habit. It is good that you practise keeping with the Light."

July 6, 1993

I am having difficulty getting going in the morning, but I am more aware of keeping the mantra with me during the day as Swami Radha instructed. We are leaving for Spokane in a few days so I have a lot to do. But this morning I go out before breakfast to pick raspberries. It is peaceful and quiet in the garden, a perfect time of day.

Later Mataji asks me, "Durgananda, what has changed?"

I am not sure what she means, but I answer, "I think I am not resisting and I am going with whatever is to be. I realize now how subtle resistance can be and how many forms it may take. It takes energy."

"Well, your face has changed and you look younger. You look at people differently."

I take her words in to reflect on later, as I am not aware of this.

"Let's walk over to the temple," she says and I support her as we go together. She pauses to look up at the dome and then steers me to the platform surrounding it. She walks slowly, pausing to look through the glass in each of the doors. Then she motions to me to open one of them and we step inside. I turn on the chandeliers for her. She sits in a chair for a while, looking up at the twinkling lights of the chandeliers, then turns to gaze through the windows. I have the feeling she is thinking about how she will be leaving the Ashram soon. The temple has a strong drawing power for her. She says quietly, "I live here."

fifteen | SURRENDER

July 11, 1993 Spokane

Yesterday I drove Mataji back to Spokane. I was aware of the tension in my driving, wanting to avoid any jiggling or bumps that might hurt her neck, but I gradually relaxed and allowed myself to drive intuitively, thinking of the protection of the Light. We saw three deer and I slowed down when they crossed the road, feeling relieved they were not too close.

Farther along, a packrat ran right toward the car and I instinctively did not swerve or jam on the brakes because of Mataji's neck, although I said a fast prayer. It was the right thing to do, as she commented on it. The packrat turned quickly and escaped.

The rest of the trip went well and we had time to unpack and settle in.

Today Mataji invites everyone from Radha House over to her apartment and treats us to pizza and wine. "I can be critical and say this or that isn't quite right, but I love you all," she says to us.

Then she tells us a story about the power of mantra. One night soon after her return from India, she was walking through a park in Montréal on her way to visit someone. She heard a man running after her. Intuitively, she stopped to take away the power and excitement of the chase. He came from behind and grabbed her by the shoulders and she said immediately to him, "First, will you do me a favour?" The man was completely surprised and said, "What do you want, money?" She told him to repeat three words, *Om Namah Sivaya*. All the while she was repeating the mantra to herself. Again she repeated to him, "*Om Namah Sivaya*." Startled, he looked at his watch and said he had to catch the last bus. Then he ran off. It was only afterward, when she analyzed her response, that she realized that by saying "first" she was partially giving consent, and that took him off guard. There was no question in her mind that his intention was rape.

She emphasizes that this happened long before she had done the lengthy mantra practices that she did in later years. "The mantra protects. It is not the hours of repetition, but the intensity of your practice and your conviction."

She gives us some advice: "If you are interested in a particular man, recite *Om Namah Sivaya* and your illusions will be stripped away and you will see him for what he really is. You have grown up thinking of the man as your protector and provider. As women, you are complete in yourselves. You do not need a man. In the sex act you lose your identity for a short time, a few seconds, but in the Kundalini experience this lasts a lot longer. So go for that experience. What happens is that we are trying to bring heaven to Earth, but we can't do that. We have to go there, to heaven, and that is what we do in Kundalini."

July 15, 1993

I am at the Ashram. A workshop for the residents is going on. Swami Radha comes in and begins teaching us Kundalini. She is able to keep going for quite awhile, then finally stops for a break. We feel very fortunate to have her teaching us.

It is reassuring to know that I am getting some teachings even in my dreams. The knowledge I gain on this level is available to me when I need it, even though I may not know where it comes from. I need to receive the teachings on all levels – through being with Swami Radha, having awareness in daily life, reading the material and doing the practices. On the subconscious level, I receive the teachings through my dreams.

July 23, 1993

I am sad to see Mataji feeling so miserable. She can't do her exercises this morning and it is even hard for her to sit through her back massage. She falls asleep during her foot massage and then goes right to bed. Later Yasoda comes over, so I do some errands. I hope I can make time to work on the drawings for the dream book.[1]

Tonight I chant softly on the sun porch, gradually wrapping a mantle of mantra around me as a protection. I vaguely hear Mataji talking to someone, I hear the phone ring, but the mantra, soft as it is, becomes foremost. Images begin to come that seem to emerge from an overactive mind and I use my will to stop them. Then the image comes to me of being on the porch at our family place on the Jersey shore – sitting alone in the fall watching the sunset. Sitting alone. Watching the sun setting over the water alone. A preparation for *sanyas*? Then images of mistakes I made during those years. I made many mistakes. But it is important to forgive myself and ask Divine Mother's forgiveness. I am clear and directed now and I don't think my mistakes are so monumental.

I think about my commitment and how I am determined to keep it. Swami Radha asked me awhile back about the commitment I made to her when she was so ill in the summer of 1988. I told her I realized how important it was for her when she was so sick to know that I wanted to give myself to her and to the teachings. That is what truly mattered to me. Another preparation for *sanyas*. I am glad I gave her that lifetime commitment.

---

1 Swami Sivananda Radha, *Realities of the Dreaming Mind: The Practice of Dream Yoga* (Spokane, WA: timeless books, 1994/2004). (The 1994 edition featured Swami Durgananda's drawings.)

July 24, 1993

Mataji asks me a question about what to wear and when I give my opinion she chooses something else. I see my ego bristle a bit and ask silently, "Why did you ask me?" Then I realize perhaps she already had something in mind and was seeing if I was sensitive enough to pick it up.

I see how quickly my ego can get in the way. Then I end up focusing on myself and my reactions, instead of getting myself out of the way. I need to listen more carefully inside and deepen my practice of surrender. Otherwise I am not doing selfless service. In so many cases when my ego interferes, I realize later how insignificant the matter is – and what difference does it make anyway?

Tonight Yasoda comes over to work on a book about Light and vibration with Mataji. This lifts Mataji's spirits. I think she forgets everything else when she starts working on her writing.

July 31, 1993

Today I enter the last year when I can say I am in my sixties. Suppose this were the last day in my life. What would I want to say? I want to say, "Thank you, Divine Mother, for my life, for a healthy body, for the protection I have had, for the teachings. Also I think of the opportunities offered me, especially for the close contact with Swami Radha and for the opportunity to serve her, to make these years as comfortable for her as I can." She has given me so much. Where would I be now if I had not had contact with her? Her teachings and her blessing have brought meaning to my life. When I run into daily irritations they are just little things that are part of living closely with someone. I don't have to take them seriously. They do show that my ego is still very much in evidence as it may feel hurt and put down. I see that there is still work to be done!

If this were the last day in my life I would feel good about my life on the whole. I have furthered my evolution although I have not achieved what I would call self-realization. I am not sure I even know what that state is.

I do feel a calm, certain connection with my Divine source. I may not always stay with it but I know it is there. I just need to lift the veil that I imagine separates me from it. I am so grateful for the guidance of the Divine, for the nudges I have received to keep me on track. I also see the power of choice. This is where free will comes in. I was brought into contact with Swami Radha but it was my choice to do something about it. I was given awareness of what the Ashram had to offer but it was my choice, my decision, to go there. Then I went through the agonizing time of assessing my role in the marriage and what my future would be, and I made a decision there, too.

When I moved into my own apartment, I felt very alone and scared, but it was my decision to move, to leave my marriage. All along I was being forced to take responsibility and to act. If I hadn't taken these steps, I think I would have ended up living a life of desperation. But the Divine was with me and I was given signs of that protection.

The decision to take *sanyas* was similar. The nagging feeling inside that there was something more to do, another step. *Come on, you are not finished, keep going, go for the highest.* Again I know something would have felt incomplete inside if I had not made that commitment.

August 3, 1993

I feel sensitive today, depleted and teary. Everything seems to touch me in a negative way. I take my emotions to the mantra. At first my mind is filled with the sensitive issues and it takes awhile to let them go. Looking at the painting of the *rasa lila* with all the peacocks fanning their tailfeathers and the *gopis* dancing with Krishna uplift me. Then I look at my picture of Durga. She is always there for me. After chanting I feel much more centred.

Getting to the bottom of what I am going through brings me to some emotions about carrying the responsibility for Swami Radha's care. This is not always easy, especially when I make a mistake. There are bits of old emotions from my childhood, feeling like a little kid who has done something wrong and is being criticized. I find it difficult to sort out what is appropriate surrender to the guru, what is unjust criticism, what is fair criticism, and what is just pickiness on my part. I feel I need to put my ego and my own feelings aside to make things as easy as possible for Mataji. I have been able to do that to a certain extent, but things just piled up today. I guess I just have a lot to learn about surrender.

August 4, 1993

I feel better today. I carried both the Rishikesh *Aarti*[2] and *Hari Om* alternating in my sleep. This has an effect.

Swami Radha receives a fax from one of the residents mentioning his practising with the finger cymbals as she instructed.

"I never told him that," she says.

I say, "Perhaps you were an instrument for the Divine and said something you don't remember now."

She replies, "Well, maybe that is why I sleep so much. My body is resting while I am zooming around." We both have a good laugh at the image that brings up.

At supper she talks about how she used to travel to "put the Ashram on the map."

"I had to sleep on lumpy mattresses sometimes." She looks over at me and I know she is referring to my switching beds because of the lumpy mattress where I was sleeping.

I reply lightly, "That is a sensitive area right now." Everyone laughs and so does she.

"Well, Durgananda slept on a chair for ten days when it really counted, while I was in the hospital." I guess that exonerates me.

She then asks people to think more deeply and question the teachings. Don't just accept what she says. Question her ideas. She turns to me and asks, "Have you found any disagreements with what I have taught you? No, don't be shy, speak up."

2   *Aarti* is a hymn sung at the opening of *satsang* to honour the Light; Swami Radha brought the Rishikesh *Aarti* back from Swami Sivananda's Ashram in Rishikesh.

I pause to think for a minute and reply, "Not in any major things but in some small things, yes."

She smiles. "Durgananda's reply shows she has been thinking deeply. She has done her reflection." I recall our disagreement about my going to my daughter's wedding. This was not actually a small thing. She hadn't wanted me to go, but when I wrote out my thoughts about it she agreed it was fine for me to go. This showed she respected my reasons. It turned out to be an important step for me in letting the family see me after my *sanyas* initiation and that I am still me.

August 11, 1993

Swami Radha thinks that I miss the Ashram and that is why I felt so down a few days ago. Now she is thinking of spending more time there. Since then, our relationship has been especially warm. I am grateful for this, as I am able to be light and have jokes with her. I assure her I am fine, but she has it in her mind now to travel to the Ashram.

I keep using the painting in my room of Krishna dancing with the *gopis*, the *rasa lila*[3] as a focus for my mantra practice. It has so many details that I can keep my mind on Krishna and feel uplifted by the meanings of the symbols.

When chanting I feel myself being drawn into the various parts of the painting, the colourful flowers, the peacocks strutting, their tail-feathers opening to reveal a thousand eyes. There is a feeling of lightness and joy. The lotus buds are swaying in the water, the cows are dancing in their clumsy way, shaking their heads in time to the music so the bells on their horns jangle and ring. The dancers move gracefully in a circle, expressing their pleasure to be with the Divine, as he appears to be dancing with each one of them at the same time. In the centre I see the Lord dancing with his true love, Radha. They reach out their hands, touching gently, then swirling and turning. Only their

3 The *Rasa* or *Krishna Lila* refers to Divine play, Krishna's dance with the *gopis*. Generally, the dance of life, the human being's dance of life with God. The *lila* is often depicted as Krishna in a circle of dancing *gopis*.

eyes connect in stillness, embracing a knowing. I feel as if I am being called. "Come join in the dance, come join with the Lord, dancing with Radha. Perhaps he will dance with you, too." I want that closeness with the Divine.

September 8, 1993

This is my initiation anniversary, nine years for mantra and four years for *sanyas*. I am happy that I awake with *Hari Om*.

In my Hatha practice I do the headstand and stay up for a long time, keeping *Hari Om* with me. It seems very easy and natural. I think, "This is not upside down. That is an illusion. Perhaps the world I normally exist in is upside down and I am used to it that way so I don't know it. But often Mataji turns things upside down to make me stretch my thinking."

She is not feeling well today. I chant for her and Sivananda, thinking of the lineage and how the work has carried on. I am so grateful for being a part of the lineage and for having the mantra initiation from Swami Radha. Tonight we have a special *satsang* for Sivananda. She tells me to attend it. She says she will feel guilty if I stay with her, because then she will have to pretend she feels better than she does. I decide to go and not stay long. I keep putting her in the Light and come back as soon as *satsang* is over.

It is hard being in the guru-disciple relationship and being responsible for the guru's care at the same time. When do I speak up and when do I keep quiet and go along with something I feel is questionable because I am learning surrender? This happens from time to time and each situation takes discrimination.

September 11, 1993

I am at the Ashram and we are planning some kind of celebration to honour Swami Sivananda. Suddenly he is here. He is very big – the expression "large as life" comes to me. He has difficulty coming up the concrete steps outside. Mataji is with him and seems to be helping him or walking with him. There is great excitement having him here.

I have two thoughts about the dream: His appearance is a confirmation for me personally of protection and guidance, and it is a message of protection for the work in general. I am thinking of the Ashram and of Mary Ann as she gets ready to take on the leadership here. Also Mataji certainly did help him by establishing the Ashram and other centres in Canada and the US.

September 14, 1993

Mataji invites me to bring my coffee to the swing on the porch. We talk a bit and then we are silent. I want to empty my mind so I can be receptive and really listen. I wonder if she might be testing me to see if I can pick up a message that she is sending me mentally. Can I tune into her thoughts? I find myself observing things outside and try not to think about what I see. I have a flash of someone raking up trash in the park. I think of the symbolism of cleaning up the trash in the inner park of my mind. But I try to wipe out all thoughts and listen, keeping the mantra in the background of my mind.

Soon I hear her breathing deeply and realize she is asleep. By this time I am experiencing a feeling of power and warmth in my solar plexus. As I focus on my heart level I am aware of an instantaneous connection moving very rapidly between the solar plexus and heart levels. As she goes deeper into sleep I begin saying the Divine Light mantra mentally, coordinating it with my breath. I visualize the Light surrounding each of us individually, then both of us together, then a shower of Light covering us completely. I alternate these images, seeing the Light coming from above and through my heart centre and creating a feeling of warmth. I feel myself filling up inside as if my spiritual tank is being filled to overflowing.

Finally she wakes up. She is surprised that she was asleep. "I slept that long?" she says when I tell her it has been almost an hour. We laugh about it and I tell her what a special time it has been for me.

September 19, 1993

Mataji has been making sure I am comfortable. This really surprises me. Usually she says we want too much comfort, but this seems to be different.

"Take what you need to be comfortable in your new place in the Ashram. You have earned it," she says with a twinkle in her eye. "Be accessible to people and if they come for help, just keep repeating *Om Namah Sivaya* and don't think about what to say. Just let it come through. If something totally unconnected comes to mind, just say it because it may be just the thing the person needs to hear." She smiles at me, the Light shining from her eyes. I feel her compassion and understanding coming through and I am aware of a softening with gratitude welling up inside of me. I know she is feeling better.

September 27, 1993

I give Mataji a foot bath, which she enjoys. Washing the guru's feet is a sacred act. It reminds me of Mary Magdalene washing the feet of Jesus and drying them with her hair.

Later I sit with her on the porch swing. She talks about Mexico and the centre she has established there.

"I feel as if I am going full circle, back to the place where I had a powerful past life. It has been important to have a centre in Mexico.[4] It can be an opening for the ones living there if they take it to heart and reflect on it."

I respond, "I wouldn't want to live there; it is too hot for me."

She looks straight at me and says, "Don't forget that you have to take the Ashram with you wherever you are." Then she adds, "I still feel very peaceful here in this apartment. It is probably the best place for me to be. I know I get too caught up at the Ashram, too many demands."

She changes the subject, "How are your drawings coming along?"

---

4   Swami Radha established a Radha Centre, Casa Radha, in Merida, Mexico, that was open from 1989 to 1996.

I tell her I have an idea for a drawing, but I need to check out some things at the library.

"You are relying on outside sources too much. You need to work from your own intuitive understanding." I do not disagree with her, although I try to explain that I get ideas that contain some elements I can't draw, like the locomotive.

"I don't go along with that. You don't trust your own ability. Do more sketches to offer choices before doing a finished drawing. Then we can look over them and decide what will work." This is a good way to loosen up my ideas.

October 10, 1993

I attended to a lot of details yesterday and this seemed to bother me. Why? Was it reminiscent of when my children were little, the kind of busy life I led?

A lot of my life situations are repeating themselves right now, but in a very different way. I have a different purpose now and I don't have to respond in the same old way. It is important to keep that clear; otherwise I get drawn back into old patterns and miss the essence of the opportunity I have. I end up selfish, wanting control, feeling self-pity, getting scattered and disorganized, wanting my own sense of peace and quiet. This is not selfless service. It keeps coming up that I need to deepen my practice of surrender.

October 21, 1993

I have removed my Egyptian ring and am looking at the inscription on the back more carefully. I realize that it is more elaborate than I thought. The inscription is written on the front of a hidden doorway. I carefully open the door and find another opening that leads into a passageway. As I investigate further, I find one ancient doorway or opening after another. I move along, not physically so much as mentally, down stone steps, along corridors, through old wooden doors that open up or out to one side or the other. All of this is on a small scale and I am following it with my mind. I am quite excited at making this discovery but I do not reach the end before I wake up (still in the dream) and tell someone what I have experienced. I am with a group of Ashram people and we are doing reflections.

This dream has a depth to it and a feeling of going back into a very ancient time as well as deep into myself. I find it difficult to describe to others in the dream. It is almost as if the repeating of the dream within the dream leads me to the next part, which has to do with reflections. So I need to reflect on it. This all emerges from my Egyptian ring, which I feel holds a secret, but I don't know what it is.

November 10, 1993

In the sitting forward bend this morning I reflect on bringing together the two parts of the body, upper and lower, and two parts of the mind. Immediately my drawings for the dream book come to mind. I see the black and white of the pen and ink drawings blending, interweaving – the conscious and the unconscious integrating. This shows me my artwork is having an effect in my body and in other areas of understanding.

Swami Radha tells me later that my patience makes her aware of her own impatience. She also refers to the time I slept in her hospital room to watch over her. She says my willingness to be ready for her at any time made quite an impression on her. For me it was an experience I will never forget. I felt like her guardian lion.

She surprises me by suggesting I drive to the Ashram in a couple of days and get settled into my new place. Then she will come with Julie a week later. Things happen so fast. What a turnaround!

November 29, 1993 Yasodhara Ashram

I join Swami Radha in her sunroom. She smiles at me. "You are moving into a new phase."

"I am not sure what you mean," I reply.

"What do you think I mean?"

"Ummm. I feel I am more accepting, that I am allowing things to unfold without worry or concern. It feels like trusting the Divine."

She says, "You seem to be pulling out of an active role in the Ashram and the Spokane centre and turning more inward. I want you to know that is the right direction. You have proved your abilities and your involvement. People won't think you are being lazy. You don't have to give up everything, just be careful. If someone asks you to do something, feel free to say, 'No, I don't think I will do that.' This is really breaking an old pattern."

It is helpful to know I am on the right track.

December 30, 1993

In the temple this afternoon, Swami Radha presents Mary Ann with the lotus ring, the symbol of the presidency of the Ashram. She tells us to support the management group by keeping them in the Light. "Don't harbour any resentments. Clear up any misunderstanding. Be courageous. Step forward. Don't start any undercurrents. And remember that your promise to the Divine is your foremost loyalty. Only that will give you eternal life. If you return to the Divine again and again, the Divine will not let you down.

"But it is important to correct your mistakes. Correcting your mistakes is perhaps the only way in which you can avoid future lives, future karma. We learn by trial and error. However, if you repeat an error knowingly, it becomes sin, and then you have something more serious to deal with. Correct it however you can. Then you will be on safe grounds. And keep your diary going. Don't forget. Reflection. Reflection. Reflection."

Her talk includes things that seem directed to individual people and their issues, but I don't think she knew about them. She has said she doesn't know sometimes why she feels moved to bring up a certain subject.

She ends by leading us through a guided meditation on the Light.

I feel very inspired. And now Mary Ann begins a new phase in her life. She will need our support.

sixteen | MOVING THROUGH OBSTACLES

January 3, 1994 Yasodhara Ashram

I am in a place where I feel inadequate around Mataji. When she asks me to find something, I get tense and make mistakes, get the wrong thing, say something inappropriate. I think I block understanding her on a different level. I slip into a low place because I let my feelings of inadequacy affect me, especially when she is critical and acts as if she can't understand how I can be so unobservant or forgetful or whatever. Why do I have these ups and downs? I want to balance them out and not be affected by external input.

January 21, 1994

For over a month now I have been in a downward spiral, not trusting myself, missing my connection to the Divine, and unsure about what my place is with Swami Radha now that I am in my own apartment and not involved with her care.

I stop by Many Mansions today to see her and to let her know what my feelings are. I feel as if I have been avoiding her. I seem to flip into an attitude of not wanting to bother her with my problems. When I say that she looks at me intensely, her eyes flashing. "Durgananda, it is not problems, it is your spiritual development."

"I know it sounds crazy, not wanting to make a mistake. I have been trying to assimilate what you said about not needing to come to you for everything now that I am more on my own."

Then she really zeroes in on me. "You have to crack the resistance of the ego or you won't make it. You chose the name of Durgananda. Durga has no consort and has to do it alone. She has to use the sword to cut away the old habits. Durga has to subdue Margaret White. The old habits stand in your way. You don't need to be so anxious about making mistakes. You get too tense. Remember we learn by trial and error. You don't want to put yourself into a prison of your own making. People admire you and there is no reason for you to hold yourself back."

There is a pause and I respond, "I am grateful for your help, Mataji. I appreciated reading in the Radha book[1] about your doubts and fears before your initiation in India. I could relate to that."

"But I hadn't been ten years in an ashram!"

I don't say anything further, as I want to stay with what she has said. I want to remember her words. I also think about the lifetimes she has had as preparation for her work this time around. They must have helped her.

She ends on a gentle note. "You may need more time, and that is all right. The lotus takes its time to open and you can't force it." I feel her kindness and compassion. This talk helps to clear the air for me and more space is opened up for the drawings as well.

I do a longer mantra practice tonight, feeling the power and how it helps to focus my mind.

January 29, 1994

After chanting and reflection in the temple with the residents this afternoon, I stop by Many Mansions. Swami Radha is just getting ready

---

1   Swami Sivananda Radha, *Radha: Diary of a Woman's Search* (Spokane, WA: time-less books, 1981/2002).

to go for a drive. She invites me to come along and I feel the heaviness lifting. It is so good to be back with her again without the contortions of my monkey mind interfering. When we get back, I wash the dishes and sweep the hall in her house to help out a little. It is as if I have moved out of some kind of limitation I had boxed myself into and am now free to come and go as I used to.

February 2, 1994

It is Mary Ann's *sanyas* initiation day! I am to initiate her. I have an auspicious dream about having a wonderful new baby, a little darker than me, perhaps with Indian blood. He seems wise for his years, with a very knowing look. It is a meaningful symbol for this day. I go over to the temple early, after talking to Divine Mother and clearing myself out of the way as much as possible. My heart is beating faster than usual and there is a feeling of excitement and anticipation. No, I just want to be a channel.

I arrange Swami Radha's and Sivananda's pictures and sit before them, thinking of absorbing their compassion and wisdom, asking the Divine to take over and use me as an instrument. And that is what happens. Mary Ann sits across from me in her blue sari. The chanting centres us and everything else flows from that. I feel supported by Swami Radha's invisible presence and I know Divine Mother is the doer, not me. It is a privilege to assist Mary Ann becoming Swami Radhananda Saraswati. At the end we hug and have our pictures taken with the other swamis.

We all go over to see Swami Radha afterward and she is full of smiles, her love for Swami Radhananda shining through her eyes.

February 13, 1994

I do an extra practice this morning, and a wonderful thing happens. I suddenly begin to experience the power and the focus of the mantra connected to each bead of the *mala* as I touch it. My mind hooks onto it and does not deviate. I feel steady and present. My word for the year, focus, is working. It feels glorious, no intruding thought, until I have a sense of Swami Radha's presence. Is she sending me Light? Is this why I am so focused? I feel as if I am in touch with her on that level.

Tonight is guru *puja*. Swami Radha arrives in a beautiful blue sari. I can see she is in pain but she seems to gain strength as she speaks. She gives an inspiring talk that touches on everything from initiation, *sanyas* and Liberation, to marriage, sex and children born out of marriage. There is something there for everyone. I am sure she is able to do this because she surrenders totally, allowing the Divine to come through her.

It is very moving to watch everyone approach her with a *pranam* and then offer a flower at her feet. I choose a red carnation that represents putting my passion into the path on which she has guided me. I want to do my very best and give from my heart. The red carnation I lay at her feet symbolizes bringing my passion to the Divine, my life blood, intensity, beauty, delicacy, softness, something that lasts, something special – to bring this to her and to all she represents. I also want to give back, to honour her work, to love, respect and bring devotion – and to know that she is the symbol for the Divine in me as well. I must remember I am giving back what the Divine has already given to me. Nothing is mine to give.

When she gets up to leave I am moved to tears – gratitude for her giving so much, sadness seeing her pain and knowing her courage, and always the concern that this might be her last *puja*. She is such a powerful symbol of true selfless service. What will we do when she is no longer with us physically?

February 20, 1994

Yesterday was quite a day. Swami Radha called asking me to bring the drawings for the dream book to Many Mansions. When I arrived she said, "I have invited a group of residents over to look at the drawings you have done. Put them on the table so everyone can look at them and give suggestions. It is helpful if other people see what you are doing."

Initially I had a strong inner reaction. *Oh, no. People won't understand what I am trying to convey.* But I silenced that voice and as I spread the drawings out on the table I asked Divine Mother to bring me the messages that would help me. After everyone arrived I noticed that Mataji quietly left the room, perhaps to lessen the pressure on me and to put the responsibility on the group for conveying their ideas.

It turned out to be a dynamic session with new concepts coming from all sides, although I began to feel overwhelmed – so many drawings would have to be changed or redone. I wrote everything down and felt very accepting of most of the ideas and grateful for the help, and not at all threatened by having everyone judging my work. It was a friendly light-hearted gathering. Getting the group together to pool ideas was Swami Radha's way of loosening me up, as I wasn't listening carefully enough to her. She is amazing!

Now I am following up today by working on some of the changes to the drawings. I can see that I had lost some of the fluidity and had become too rigid and literal. I wonder if I was getting caught in the trap of black-and-white thinking (like the black-and-white drawings I am doing) instead of playing around with them.

I make the images more flowing and that brings in a very different quality. I look at the pictures that need changing to see if there is something that relates to me and my life. The most obvious one is the "Value of Dreams." I really liked the idea I had but it kept changing as I sketched it. I ended up with something that was not right but I didn't know why, so I put it away and avoided working on it. It is a male figure standing at the entrance to a hallway with a series of doors leading to the Light. He is observing. But someone said he looks sinister, waiting in the shadows, holding back. I was shocked at first, then wondered if this was why I hadn't felt right about it. When I redo it this morning I make a very feminine, flowing figure moving toward the Light-filled room at the end. It brings a much lighter feeling and makes a tremendous difference.

So who is this sinister male aspect in me? Is it the critical judge that hangs back in the shadows waiting to attack me if I make a mistake – a so-called mistake in his eyes? He doesn't look fierce; he looks like a normal everyday guy, but this can be deceiving. I connect this aspect of myself with the thinking, reasoning part that I often put down in my past. This part of me could not make itself heard or understood and it gradually withdrew into the shadows. But it now comes out in a burst of arrogance or resentment picked up from those old days. It feels very good to take him out of the picture and to replace him with a graceful feminine figure going toward the Light.

I stop by to tell Mataji how much I appreciate her help in getting me unstuck. She reminds me, "Now remember, for your drawing of the mystical union you have to start with what it means to you. Where would mystical union take place for you? That is the most important thing. Don't look at how other people would portray it or get ideas from other sources."

I already have some ideas that have come to me for the section she is talking about and I will sketch them today while they are fresh in my mind.

April 3, 1994

Swami Radha calls me over to Many Mansions to look at the designs for the dream book cover. I really listen to what she says, and when we are finished I show her my ideas for drawings as yet undone to get more input.

She looks at what I have done, then smiles and says, "Well, you got there." Wow! By listening to her and surrendering my way, I have loosened up and succeeded in getting where she has been directing me. I have had to expand my mind to fit her idea of the chapter I am illustrating. The drawings are often on my mind. Images come to me as I go to sleep and as I awake. How do I avoid bringing in my self-will, my self-expression? I reflect on surrender and self-will.

I think about pride, sorting out pride in a job well done from unhealthy pride that comes from my ego and is an obstacle. Pride protects my ego from the threat of criticism. Pride clings to my ego and creates a separation from my Divine source. The way back to a connection is through surrender. Surrender is the softening of the rigidity of pride.

I need to keep taking each action back to the purpose of it. Why am I doing it? With the drawings I am trying to bring my awareness to the meaning behind the idea, to the Light. Take it back to the Light. Offer it up to the Light. Then let it go.

April 9, 1994

Chanting in the temple this morning, softly, gently, feeling the longing. Even knowing the Divine is with me, within me, the longing is still there. I keep coming to the Divine, calling. Yet the Divine is always there. I just don't remember, I don't recognize that reality. Why can't I shift into that reality and *be* it? Just keep with it. Someday I will make it, someday.

After lunch I stop in to see Swami Radha. She says, "So here is the recluse." She hasn't seen me for a while, yet now I can relax instead of being uptight about whether she expected me to stop in or not, whether I should or shouldn't. My monkey mind.

I ask her if it is all right to chant more than one mantra now.

She says, "Siva is the Lord of Yoga, so he would be addressed when doing yoga." So I figure that *Om Namah Sivaya* is more appropriate to use in Hatha classes.

But she continues, "I have also used *Hari Om* in my classes as well as *Om Namah Sivaya*. Think about it as addressing different aspects of a person, like mother or daughter or teacher or wife; or calling them by different parts of their name. When I met you Peggy was the name you used. Then it was Margaret, then you became Swami Durgananda. But it is the same person." So I understand that it is all right to chant to Siva at times in my practice.

Again she mentions my withdrawing from people and activities. She asks, "How old are you now?"

"I will be seventy in July." I can hardly believe this myself.

"Well, you are a people person, but you can't take people with you when you leave the Earth plane. You need to prepare for the transition."

When she says this I feel the ego needs to drop away. It is important to focus on my inner development and let go of the stuff that pulls me down.

April 18, 1994

Walking to the temple in the morning is now part of my practice. It is a time of being with the mantra, taking in the surroundings, the mountains, trees, birds. I see the swallows today for the first time this spring. As I walk I look forward to my Divine appointment.

During chanting I feel myself slipping into a trance-like state and I don't want to lose awareness this way, so I open my eyes and focus on the flame of the oil lamp. In the centre of it I see what looks like an old sage in robes, sitting and nodding to me. I watch for a while and then close my eyes. When I open them again he is gone.

I end my chanting by sitting under the centre of the dome and have a sense of myself being drawn up and up, opening out into space. Yet I have such a connection with the temple that it draws me into myself as well.

Later I talk to Swami Radha about my brother's memorial service. His family is having it in June at their summer place in Connecticut. Even though he died last November, they wanted to have a service for him in the summer. "I don't want the family to think the Ashram is preventing me from going, but I need to stay here to keep my focus on my practices. What I have started is important. I don't want it interrupted at this point."

She nods approval and says, "We can have a service of Light in the temple and honour him in that way."

That feels like the right thing to do and I will plan something that is simple, something he could relate to. This is how I want to honour my brother. But it will be hard for the family to understand.

I also show her my dream book drawings, giving her a choice. I am surprised at her choices, but then everyone who has seen them has chosen something different. Swami Radha says not to choose the one that gets the most votes or the least votes. I guess this means to stay with the middle way. Or is she telling me to use my intuition?

She asks if there is anything I need from her before she leaves for Spokane in the next day or two. Then she gives me another project to work on. She says she doesn't want me "to get lazy." And she laughs.

As I leave I tell her about going to the temple every morning to chant. "It has become an important part of my day. I feel that the walk there is part of my practice." She smiles. "Like a pilgrimage," she says, and that is what it feels like.

May 8, 1994 Spokane

I am in Spokane giving a workshop over the weekend. Wendy calls me for Mother's Day. She tells me she had a very vivid dream about a month ago in which I came to visit her. She hugged me and it seemed very real. She said in the dream, "You aren't really here, are you?" and I replied, "No, I'm not." Then I expressed concern for Carla and we talked about her. Then I was gone. She felt very happy when she woke up.

When I tell Swami Radha about it later she says, "Do you see now why I pushed you so hard? But you have to expand this to other people in need of help."

"But shouldn't I know when this happens?"

"Not necessarily, but sometimes you will know."

She also says, "I knew you didn't like it when I came down hard on you but I could see you took it and applied it to other areas. That showed you understood."

She becomes serious for a moment and talks about something that has obviously been on her mind. She says the use of "Mataji" has become too casual. It is a term of great respect and implies a very serious commitment by the person who uses it. I think many people have been using it as an ordinary form of address and this is not right. She wants us to use "Swami Radha" from now on. It sounds more formal to me but I understand why she is doing this and I honour her reasons. I will have to get used to it, as I have called her Mataji for over twelve years.

September 1, 1994 Spokane

I am here with the management group from the Ashram, visiting Swami Radha. She has a lot of directions for everyone, including me.

"Do you have one last desire left?" she asks.

I try to think but cannot come up with any. Then I say, "I used to want to go to Egypt, but don't really feel I need to do that anymore."

Immediately she responds, "Yes, that is it." I think she feels I am giving a message by wearing the scarab necklace she gave me recently. "I don't want you to move on carrying that desire with you. I don't want you to have to come back for another lifetime because of a desire that was not fulfilled. It is all right for you to go to Egypt."

I am really surprised at this and thank her. I wonder if she thinks I may recall the past life I had in Egypt with her if I go there. Should I take this as a sign to go or should I wait for my own understanding to bring me a message when I am ready? She is kind and full of Light. It is a joy to be with her again.

September 2, 1994

I have breakfast with Swami Radha, sitting across from her at her desk. She looks straight at me and I know this is an important time. She gets right to the point.

"Durgananda, you have some bad habits. Being undisciplined. Wanting to be around people. Wanting to be constantly confirmed by being with people. But it is time now for you to be a friend to yourself. Go through your diaries. What is there left to do? Take care of unfinished business. Take stock and go over your life. Create a spiritual atmosphere wherever you are. Think of the Divine being with you no matter what you are doing, even going to the bathroom. You chose the name Durgananda for a reason. You knew why you needed that name. Use it!

"Let go of not trusting yourself. Get your own experiences and come from that place of knowing. I have more trust in you than you have in yourself! You have not fully accepted your potential. In fact, you don't really have an idea of what your potential is. You need to accept the guru within yourself. Always remember you are a *sanyasin* of the Saraswati Order and live up to that."

She pauses to sip her coffee and I ask, "Should I resign my official positions with the Ashram organizations?"

"Yes, this would be best for you. You want to take the time that remains to prepare yourself so when death comes you will know it is just stepping from one room into another. It isn't enough just to imagine that it will happen this way. You have to do the work. You may have twenty years left, but you may have only ten."

She tells me that I can't just daydream about death being like walking through a door and think it will happen that way. I have to make the experience real through doing the practices – the Divine Light Invocation, the mantra. That will create a real connection that I can know in myself, not just wishful thinking, skimming the surface. That's why she wants me to take time to focus on the spiritual practices.

Then she moves on to self-expression. "What is self-expression? Who or what wants to express itself? Why would you want to waste your time on getting involved in external activities when you don't need that anymore? You don't need to be in the kitchen. You don't even need to teach. Why would you want to go back to kindergarten when you are already in the twelfth grade? You don't need to rely on the approval of other people. What difference does it make what people think?

"I have seen that you do not resist the suggestions I make, and you have read the Eastern texts without needing prodding. The challenges I give you now are to make you get past the obstacles, to get you moving. You have spent many years as an ordinary wife and you have to understand that and be gentle with yourself. You are a kind and considerate person.

"You need to get control of the personality aspects one by one. Durgananda has to take Peggy by the hand and tell her she will be shown what to do. Remember that Durga is the one who has no male consort; she has to do it alone."

I listen carefully, trying to take it all in. I sense that it has been hard for her to challenge me because she might be risking our friendship. She has mentioned before that we have been together a long time and that I have really stayed with my commitment. But this talk forces me to look at what I have and what I have been given, and to live up to that without holding back.

When I say goodbye I come around to her side of the desk and she turns her chair to look at me. I kneel in front of her and bring my hands to *namaste,* looking deeply into her eyes. She smiles and says gently, "When you have children you have to prepare them for life. When you have spiritual children you have to prepare them for spiritual life so if they do have to come back again, they will have a good life. Give me a kiss." Tears fill my eyes as I give her a kiss and thank her.

September 8, 1994 Yasodhara Ashram

Today is Sivananda's birthday and also my birthday, ten years for mantra and five years for *sanyas.* Doing the Sun Salutations I focus on giving birth to inner stillness, which is what I want to emerge more and more. To stand alone, full of Light and strength, to give to others from that place, from inner stillness, rather than always thinking "I have to do." Reaching to the Light, bowing down in humility and gratitude. Help me, Divine Mother.

Conquest of self is arduous. Focus on faith and recognize that faith is a power in itself. Have faith that I will make it. Have faith in Swami Radha. She leaves me with hope. Have faith in her trust in me. Have faith in my Divine spark.

November 10, 1994 Spokane

I have come to Spokane to help care for Swami Radha.

The first night here with Swami Radha goes smoothly. We are sleeping in the living room. Swami Radha is on an inclining chair that is more comfortable for her, keeping her head elevated. I am nearby on the couch. Swami Radha sleeps very well but only for two-hour stretches, so we are up several times in the night, usually for an hour or two each time. Sometimes I don't go back to sleep right away so I do *Japa,* repeating the mantra silently. Toward morning I go into a deeper sleep and then have difficulty waking up.

At breakfast Swami Radha says, "I was concerned that you would not be able to handle the night shift, that it might be too much for you. It is wonderful that you are doing so well."

For my part, I feel it has not been hard at all, at least so far. I am so happy to be close to her once more. It is hard to see her suffering, but I will help her in whatever way I am asked.

November 18, 1994

It has been a very difficult time. Swami Radha has been in a lot of pain from her arthritis. I was not with her last night as I attended the book launch for *Realities of the Dreaming Mind* at the library. When I returned, she was feeling miserable.

As I helped her to bed I prayed to Divine Mother to give her some relief. She had a relatively smooth night with less pain and we did get some sleep. She was fine today, but tonight had another miserable evening. Julie and I are desperate, trying to think of ways to help her. We watched a video on the royal family and it's now 3:00 a.m.

She tells me that the pain makes her irritable. I understand completely. She is concerned that I'm not getting enough rest and suggests I take turns in the night with someone else so I can get more sleep.

It has been quite a learning experience to observe her. I see the Divine spark in her so clearly. Even in times of pain she is able to shift into a different level of consciousness. Her mind becomes sharp and clear. She is able to talk about all kinds of ideas. She gives me guidelines for the prayer list. She stops me when I am reading aloud to her and begins a long exposition about some of the ideas in the book. This is put onto tape. I feel like a sounding board for her and am only able to ask a few questions. At other times she dozes off in her chair and looks so frail.

December 4, 1994

Swami Radhananda has been here for a few days visiting Swami Radha. This morning Swami Radha is not feeling well and tells us we should go back to the Ashram. I guess she settled some Ashram affairs with Radhananda and thought it best for her to get back. I go back with her and hope that Swami Radha will feel well enough to come with Julie for Christmas.

December 24, 1994 Yasodhara Ashram

I lead the chanting in the temple this morning. It is wonderful to have the huge Christmas tree full of lights, the focus of our decorations this year.

In the afternoon the residents meet to chant and have some treats and read our Christmas stories. Each person has chosen a character from the story of the birth of Jesus in the New Testament, and written about the birth of the Christ child from that perspective. In the evening, Swami Radhananda leads *satsang*. Each person reads a short saying of Swami Radha's, and we sing Christmas carols and *bhajans*.

After *satsang* the phone rings. I answer it. Swami Radha is calling from Spokane. She is feeling better but has decided not to come to the Ashram as planned. I have been concerned about her traveling and think that it is best for her to stay there where it is quiet, but we will miss her.

Before going to bed I sit quietly in the Lotus pose. I have a sense of a bud located in my heart centre, opening gradually and releasing warmth that radiates outward. I have a feeling that what I am struggling to achieve is really very simple; I don't need to struggle. The lotus is the same as space; the breathing spirit and the sun go forth to greet each other. I make space for the breathing spirit to breathe me, for the light of the solar fire to warm me, enter and fill me. Words, what do they mean now?

seventeen | CHALLENGES

January 14, 1995 Yasodhara Ashram

Swami Radha is talking to me very directly about getting in touch with her. She likes to hear from me now that she is in Spokane. I tell her I have written to her even if I haven't phoned. She is smiling. I feel I am in touch with her even when I haven't literally been talking to her on the phone.

"Durgananda! Swami Radha is on the phone. She wants to talk to you."

I pick up the phone and am surprised when she says, "You and I have been meeting."

Does she know about my dream? I say, "Yes, do you come here or do I go there?"

She replies, "You come here." And then she asks, "How would you like to come down to Spokane and help out here?"

I pause, thinking of my teaching obligations, and tell her I am sure I can make arrangements. She tells me to come as soon as possible.

January 16, 1995 Spokane

Swami Radhananda drives me to Spokane so she can visit with Swami Radha. We talk about what selfless service really is. She tells me a great story.

The devotee brings the guru some tea. The guru tastes it and says, "It's too hot. Take it back and cool it off." When the devotee returns the guru tastes it again. "Now it's too cool. Warm it up." The devotee returns once again. "It needs more sugar." The next time, "This cup is too hard for me to handle. Get a different one." And on and on. Can the disciple respond and do what is asked without getting irritated and questioning why this is happening? If yes, it is selfless service. If no, a wonderful opportunity has been lost to learn something valuable from the guru.

When we arrive, Swami Radha greets us warmly. I will be helping Julie and Arnon, but tonight I just observe the routine so I may learn quickly what she needs. Arnon is on night duty. She has a quiet way about her and is very methodical. I feel at ease, as she has a great sense of humour that lightens things up. Tomorrow I start on the night shift.

January 17, 1995

Swami Radhananda has a long talk with Swami Radha about the Ashram and possible directions. Some of the ideas seem quite radical, but then so did the silent meals when that was first put into effect. When I talk to Swami Radhananda later she says she listens to what Swami Radha says and surrenders to that because she wants to learn from Swami Radha's experience and wisdom.

Tonight I help Arnon with Swami Radha's care. Then I prepare my sleeping space. I put a foam pad on the floor at the foot of Swami Radha's bed. It is just wide enough to fit between the bed and a table that holds a shrine with an image of Tara, the Tibetan goddess of compassion. It is a powerful location, lying between Swami Radha and Tara. I feel the significance of lying at the guru's feet as if, in a sense, I am the watchdog. And I feel in turn watched over by Tara. But also I have a feeling I can't put into words that there is a significance about being in this particular position, lying perpendicular to her feet.

I repeat the Divine Mother prayer often as I get used to this new position. The first time I help Swami Radha get up, her neck is sore and she chokes swallowing a pill. That is scary. But the rest of the night all goes smoothly. I begin to feel back in the swing of things. It was different two years ago when I slept in the next room and Swami Radha was able to get up on her own in the night.

It must be difficult for her to rely on her disciples for so many personal services, some that a nurse would be able to do more efficiently and impersonally. But she is willing to give us this opportunity to face ourselves as she presents lessons in awareness, selfless service, consideration, respect. I have a new appreciation for the depth of her compassion.

January 20, 1995

As Swami Radha takes a nap I sit quietly visualizing the Light and repeating *Hari Om*. It is good practice. Later there is great excitement as the video team returns from their work at the local cable station. Deborah and Charles are getting training, planning programs and interviews, doing the filming and editing until the final product is broadcast locally. They show us their latest program. Swami Radha is pleased with how well it turned out and talks about ideas for future videos.

She turns to me and asks, "Well, Durgananda, what suggestion do you have?"

I have been turning over an idea in my mind for a while and am enthusiastic about it, so here is the opportunity to bring it forward.

"I think it would be great to follow up the interview on dreams with something on symbolism." I am thinking about symbolism as one of the basic elements in Swami Radha's teachings, especially in the Kundalini system.

Swami Radha looks sternly at me. "People aren't interested in symbolism. You can't produce just what you want. You have to appeal to the audience. No one is interested in art. Just because you are an artist doesn't mean other people are." I am stunned and can feel myself sinking into an old place, withdrawing and becoming silent and feeling very small.

My mind churns. Why did she come on so strongly? It doesn't make sense. She didn't even give me a chance to explain what I meant. Resentment rises up and I am mired in old emotions – familiar feelings of inadequacy and being put down. I ask myself: Where does this come from? I remember my mother's oversensitivity, seeing her withdraw into a silent moody place to hide her anger or resentment. I see myself doing the same thing. Patterns repeating from one generation to another. But I thought I had pulled out of this. Why am I still sinking into this murky, muddy place?

I remain silent. It is better than saying something I will regret later. The conversation goes on to other ideas. I feel my ego nursing its hurt image of itself. Ah! My ego is bruised. Did she do this to make me aware of the ego and how easily it is hurt? I have a choice. I silently repeat the Divine Mother prayer to shift out of the negative frame of mind.

Sometimes Swami Radha has to exaggerate my weaknesses and faults so that I get the message and do something about it. Of course, she takes a risk that I may get upset, that my pride may prevent me from looking deeper; and that I may walk away. There are others who have done this. I don't want to fall into that trap. I hope I have learned from this experience.

Later I remember two things Swami Radha said shortly after I arrived at the Ashram.

"Living in a situation that has an effect on your sense of self-worth and dignity is something you have to deal with. Otherwise, you may end up hurting yourself and damaging your self-image."

In the situation with Swami Radha, a different element is present, that of the guru teaching the disciple a lesson. She has to take advantage of any situation that is presented to her to get a message across to me, even exaggerating to make it more obvious.

I also remember her saying this: "Don't feel hurt when someone puts you down. This is self-inflicted hurt. Toughen up. You have to examine your pride and use the process of reasoning to do away with unnecessary hurts. You have to be able to take criticism and that includes even unjust criticism."

In this exchange she has helped me to see how my ego responds and my pride is affected. What a sense of freedom there is in not having to play the game any more, if I can be aware.

January 23, 1995

Early this morning I make a mistake. I heat Swami Radha's soup and test it before giving it to her. It doesn't feel hot to me but it burns her tongue. She is disgusted and says she just wants to go back to bed. I feel badly and recall the story Swami Radhananda told about the disciple serving tea to the guru. I should have considered that she might be more sensitive to heat than I am. Why didn't I think of that? It shows me how very aware I must be in every detail. I don't want to remain upset, as it is important not to project my emotions, especially as they might affect her.

Deborah speaks to me about Swami Radha's challenge to me about the video ideas. She feels Swami Radha was trying to get a message across to her about being self-willed and controlling, the way Swami Sivananda scolded Swami Radha in order to get a message across to someone else. Swami Radha has explained this as the daughter being scolded to give the daughter-in-law a message. Deborah and I decide that it really doesn't matter who the message was meant for since we both have learned something from it.

Later I am sitting on the swing in the enclosed porch doing some sewing when Swami Radha joins me. I am surprised. In the kitchen, I had seen the schedule for the three of us who care for her. By my name it said "Swami Durgananda 10:00 p.m. to 6:00 a.m." I am not scheduled for any time during the day. I immediately assumed that she doesn't want me with her as much and doesn't want me preparing any of her meals. I assumed she is disappointed in me for my carelessness with the soup.

She asks, "Is there anything you need, Durgananda? I feel you are getting tired. I can see it in your face, and I don't want it to keep building up. I wouldn't want you to get more and more tired." I do not feel disappointment from her, only warmth and compassion. She smiles and continues, "Then I might drain energy from you, or you might drain energy from me, without either of us knowing it. So I think you should be on fewer hours."

She has also arranged for me to take naps where I won't be disturbed. Then she mentions the book cover I am designing.

"I can see that you have become stronger and no longer feel rejection if your ideas aren't necessarily right. I think you understand the need for having lots of ideas and doing some brainstorming. So do a variety of sketches and we can go over them and choose the best."

I hear the genuine concern in her voice and agree that all this will be fine.

January 29, 1995

During the night, Swami Radha speaks to me about energy.

"Durgananda, you need to be clear about where you want to put your energy. If you do things that have more of an external focus, you will be drawn away from a focus on inner work. The practices are most important at this stage of your life. The design work is okay to do provided you bring the inspiration from inside and connect with the Most High.

"You need to take the next two years to do whatever you can to conclude any desires or unfinished business. If you don't make it in this life, you may not have another chance because it is the end of the Kali *Yuga*."[1]

That sounds serious and I want to do as much as I can.

"Do the Divine Light Invocation and then sit down and reflect on what it really means – 'I am created by Divine Light.' Then do the

---

1 In the Indian tradition, there are four descending stages of development referred to as *yugas*. The fourth is the Kali *Yuga*, the one in which we are now living. It is said that in the first *yuga* people are perfectly virtuous, and in the last *yuga* people have forgotten virtue almost entirely.

practice of the pinpoint of Light moving up the spine.[2] This practice will take care of a lot of work. It will make quite a difference."

February 2, 1995

Today we have a guru *puja* to celebrate Swami Radha's initiation day. Followers from the surrounding area gather to pay their respects. Swami Radha gets things going immediately by calling the initiates up one by one and asking us what initiation means to us. When it is my turn she asks me, "Durgananda, tell us what initiation means to you."

I come closer and kneel in front of her. "For me initiation means responsibility – to the teachings, to you, to the Divine – to follow through, to put all the effort I can into achieving self-realization. This means commitment. Also, I would be very sad if you had to come back for another life because I failed in my commitment."

She tells us that an initiation is placed within the length of time of the Yuga it is given in. "That could be as many as 400,000 human lives, so that can mean a lot of karma. This is the last of the four Yugas, so that can mean you'll never have another chance. Sivananda said, 'No more births for Radha.' That means I am the last. Naturally, it had to be earned. Nothing is ever given on a silver platter. Many limited minds have passed through the Ashram. When people like that get something genuine, they don't recognize it and they can't take care of it."

I say that I don't know how much karma I brought in, and what I have to clear away.

"It's an effort. Keep going. You can pray for an extension of your life till you reach that goal, if it's not for pleasure that you want to live but because you want to reach your goal. Then you must take care of your health. And be courageous. You have to initiate more people. Let me make a comparison. The experience of marriage can be important, but you don't have to marry a billionaire. See what I mean? In an initiation you give whatever you can."

---

2   This visualization is described on p. 256 of *Kundalini Yoga for the West.*

I am very touched by what she has said. I feel fortunate that I have been given a healthy body and I don't want to take it for granted.

We offer flower petals at her feet and she follows this with a talk on sacrifice. She says the flowers we offer are really a symbol of an offering of ourselves. My spiritual tank feels filled after today.

February 17, 1995

In the middle of the night we watch the final act of Wagner's opera, *Lohengrin*. I think about the message of the myth. It has to do with trusting the Divine and not testing the Divine purpose or plan. Pride, self-will and listening to the ego's voices ruin the heroine's chance of union with the Divine, the higher self.

When it is over Swami Radha talks about her own tests and how she handled one that happened before going to India.

"The week before I went to India a co-worker invited me for a farewell dinner. When I arrived, her brother was there. I had met him before. While my friend was in the kitchen, he told me that I was foolish to go to India like this without knowing what was in store. He told me he had always known that I would make him a wonderful wife. He said we could travel together and I could have whatever I wanted, as he was a multimillionaire.

"You see the trap, here? So I thanked him and said I had to go to India to find out for myself. Then he said, 'All right. But when you are ready to come back, I will await a phone call or a telegram from you – reverse the charges – and I will meet you in Cairo, all expenses paid. We can get married there and stay in the hotel right by the pyramids. And then we can travel wherever you want.' This was a test, a temptation to have everything taken care of. But I held on to my faith of knowing what was right for me, and that was going to Sivananda.

"Now in *Lohengrin* there are several places where Elsa, the heroine, has a chance to reverse her doubts and show her faith so the situation could have been set right, but she doesn't do it. The Divine will give us chances to reverse our wrong decisions or wrong actions, but if we miss those opportunities then we have sealed our fate."

February 22, 1995

A young woman is using her training in spiritual disciplines to begin helping others through the powers she has developed. She is new at this, a bit unsure of herself, yet there is a strength that comes through. I am observing her.

This must be a new emerging aspect of myself. Right now I feel I am regressing because I haven't been doing the practices I used to do at the Ashram. And yet I feel a deepening of my practice of surrender, of my acceptance of where I am and how to just be in the present moment. So maybe I am moving into a deeper understanding of selfless service.

I pick up clues from Swami Radha by being very aware of what she says. I observed that she doesn't like dirty dishes or glasses on her desk so I make sure I take them away when she is finished with them. But now she has made remarks that tell me I have carried this too far, that I need to pull back and not overdo it.

Swami Radha keeps up with the news on TV each day but I know she watches it in a different way, observing the body language, the functioning of the mind, and other things that develop her awareness more. She reminds me: "One thing you can do when watching the news is to put suffering people into the Light. That is how we can be of service. I also watch the news to be informed about places I have been in, whether it is in this life or a previous one."

She adds, "You need to develop your sense of touch more by not relying on your sight so much. Close your eyes and listen to what the people say on TV and you will get a different message than relying just on sight."

It feels a bit odd to be sitting beside her with my eyes closed when she is watching TV but I want to practise what she suggests. Touch has to do with what I feel when I hear the person talking. I know that I use my sense of touch more than sight when I walk backward with her holding my wrists for support, guiding me, feeling my way rather than seeing. I guess listening with my eyes closed develops my sense of hearing as well.

After a full day today I am tired and ready for a rest, but Arnon, Julie and Yasoda are not available. Being there when needed brings up my training as a mother. I see that the experience of having had children, who require constant attention, gives me the kind of stamina and dedication that I need now. There were times when several members of the family were sick at once and I was up and down stairs, getting juice, making soup, waiting on them all and going full tilt until bedtime, and then being on call in the night. It was just part of the job. But it was also a solid preparation for Karma Yoga in the future. So as time passes and Swami Radha stays up, I find my energy flowing back as if I am given what I need as I need it.

We go to bed around midnight, but I can't get to sleep. Swami Radha goes to sleep as soon as her head touches the pillow. Is this because of her degree of surrender in other areas? Is she able to let go of any thoughts and surrender to sleep immediately? Or does her body just respond instantly to the need for sleep?

February 28, 1995

This has been a very difficult night. Swami Radha wakes up at 11:30 and is cold, but her stomach is sensitive so she doesn't want any weight on it. Her sweater is too heavy. She asks what coverings are available. Not much seems to be here. It turns out that what she wants is the comforter I have been using since I arrived.

I say, "I can use the one off the bed in the other room."

She replies intensely, "I can't use this one until it is neutralized, otherwise I would pick up your stuff. People use my things without any thought and I have no privacy. It seems that anything I have can be used by anyone. I wondered about people calling me Mataji as it seems to have no meaning. Calling me Swami Radha gives a little distance and perhaps more respect." After a pause she adds, "Familiarity breeds contempt."

I say nothing. My mind is racing. I am reacting inside. My ego wants to defend itself. When I stop to think about it I could have checked with her before using the comforter or just brought something with me for my own use. I mustn't assume anything. I need to think for myself and be sensitive to the ramifications of my actions. I must remember that Swami Radha has developed tremendous sensitivity through the practices she has done over the years. Also, now that she is not feeling well, I think her sensitivity is increased.

Later, reflecting on her phrase "familiarity breeds contempt," I think it refers to people who have no foundation in a relationship but who behave as if they do. I have known Swami Radha for many years and have always felt a deep caring and respect for her. But as I think about her words, I know I have to take them in for myself. The danger of familiarity goes deeper than just my use of her comforter. I think about the times when I sink into those negative places, become irritated with her and criticize her in my thoughts. I know she can pick up what is going on in my mind because she has done this many times. If I cannot control my mind and my ego as she has been teaching me, there is a great risk of hurting her and of spoiling our relationship. There are many intimate times with her that are very precious to me. They are experiences that I hold in my heart. They form the tapestry of our relationship that has been woven into something very dear to me. How could I risk spoiling all this through careless actions or thoughts?

She did not create the separation I am feeling now; I created it. It is like the separation from the Divine: it is not the Divine that separates from me, it is my actions or attitudes that separate me from the Divine. I need to consider what I do to my higher self, my Divine nature, when I am selfish, forgetful or self-willed, or when I gossip, express criticism, pass judgement or otherwise indulge in negative emotions. These damage my inner Self, and what great pain there is in that. It is within my power to avoid such states or turn them around.

Remember I am serving Divine Mother when I serve my Guru.

March 1, 1995

Yesterday I located a quilt to use on my bed. The comforter will be dry cleaned and the cover washed. I will pay for it, to make up for my carelessness.

Last night was another difficult night. Swami Radha is still angry with me. I can't let the silent treatment go on without saying something. So when she gets up, I approach the subject.

"Swami Radha, I am sorry about the comforter and I will pay for the dry cleaning."

"That is not the point. You know I travel with my own bedding because of the vibrations. It isn't right that I don't have any privacy in my own place. I am not being respected."

I understand what she is saying and wish I could do something. I respond lamely, "I know it is not right. I realize I should have used something else."

There isn't anything else I can say. I keep *Hari Om* going and make an effort to be agreeable and to listen to her, doing what she asks. I bring her pea soup with her vitamin C but she doesn't drink it. I must have made a mistake there, assuming she would want this because she has in the past. I tell myself silently, "Don't make assumptions."

I must listen more carefully and reflect on where I haven't listened. I am still careless, thoughtless and selfish. How can I make amends? Saying I am sorry is not enough. Under these circumstances I feel that Swami Radha does not want me around, as my presence must distress her. This pain feels like the pain of separation from the Divine.

This feeling of separation is important for me to experience. Unless I have felt something, I don't really know what it is like. And separation from the Divine is similar. It means I need to take action. In this case I think I handled it as well as I could at the time by coming to her and telling her how I felt. But I could also have mentioned that if she preferred being alone I would be in the kitchen. She could call me if she needed anything. This is being honest and direct.

Tonight I feel sadness flood over me again. I can't just ignore it. I want to express it somehow to Swami Radha. I kneel beside her at her desk and all I can say is, "I am sorry, Mataji." I meant to say Swami Radha but Mataji just came out. I put all my feeling into those few words. Then I prostrate to her. How else can I show my feelings? Sorrow, humility, gratitude, all mixed together. She looks at me intensely and turns back to her desk. I remain in the background after that, but I notice a change. She asks me to get her some milk and I feel something has been dropped. Perhaps she accepts my expression of regret and a healing can happen.

March 3, 1995

Swami Radha is not alienated from me anymore, but I still reflect on what I learned from the incident. I am writing things down as they come to me, and the list is growing. There is a tremendous learning here and I will write a paper about it to give to her.

Do I not listen? I have some examples of where I have listened and have responded from that place of awareness; but I must be missing something because I am getting the message that I am not listening. I know when my mind is busy I don't listen well. I want to listen more carefully and be more attentive. I must quiet my mind.

Where am I selfish? I don't like to look at this. Did my desire for comfort play a role? The situation involved a comforter. That is symbolic. Do I want comfort more than I think I do? And am I careless and thoughtless? I need to look at being inconsiderate because this connects with not thinking things through, not considering the implications of my actions.

Am I arrogant? I don't want to be arrogant. False pride gets in the way and I make excuses. Even if I don't verbalize them I think them in my mind. Negative emotions come up. I am not taking responsibility. I need to let go of wanting to be right, saving face. I want to take responsibility for my actions and practise humility. When gratitude and humility are in my heart, the negative qualities will drop away. It is painful to know I hurt my Guru. I feel overwhelming sadness.

I feel empowered when I see how false pride connects to hurt feelings, resistance and other emotions. Feeding into that negative state only strengthens those personality aspects. Learning the signs of falling into the trap helps me to make a conscious decision to change my behaviour pattern.

I am glad I have done reflections, as they have laid a foundation for understanding the obstacles that interfere with true surrender. I was caught in an emotional reaction and the reflections have showed me the way out.

March 4, 1995

Swami Radha has an appointment at the hairdresser this morning so I decide to clean up around, under and on top of her desk while she is gone. I do it as an act of total awareness. As I do each thing I ask myself, "Have I placed this item back where it was? Have I dried the surfaces that were damp from the cloth? Have I left her chair as I found it?" No, I left it facing the desk instead of facing out ready for her to sit down. This would be an inconvenience for her. Is there anything I can do to help her without her having to ask me? Yes, fold more tissues and put them where she can reach them. Empty the scrap basket. Fill her little dish with corn flakes. Do each thing with care and attention. Remember to leave the glasses that have something in them. Remove the empty ones. All of these little actions take awareness and consideration.

When she gets back she is not feeling well so she goes to bed. She is still edgy. All of this is a good lesson in selfless service. Do I want to serve only when everything is smooth and pleasant, or am I willing to serve when there are challenges and I don't get approval or acceptance?

In spite of the challenges, I can see the progress I have made since I helped with Swami Radha's care two years ago. I have no desire to be with the others. I am quieter inside and more focused on Swami Radha's well-being.

March 5, 1995

Swami Radha tells me she is very pleased that I wrote the paper.

"We think we know ourselves, but really we know very little," she says. Then she gives me a specific example to help make me more aware. "Do you remember a few weeks ago when you tried to take off my earrings as I was getting ready for bed? You forced a part of them and broke the stem so I had to have them repaired."

I remember. The clasp on those earrings was difficult. I don't wear earrings so I have no idea how they work. What were my options? To ask if she has another, similar pair and can show me how they work? To look at the earrings more closely and ask myself, "What part is the clip? What do I pull down? How does this work?" I wonder why I have such resistance to the whole idea of pierced ears; I have always thought that if Divine Mother had wanted us to have a hole in our ears, She would have made them that way.

The first time I help Swami Radha get up tonight, I do it wrong and upset her sensitive neck. It is a disaster. I think back to how it worked before. I finally remember that I used both my hands under a pillow lower down on her back. This works and all is well from then on. But why couldn't I remember that in the very beginning? Is it that I don't maintain a clear focus or is my memory simply not clear?

After using the pillow on her back to get her up, even though it works, she tells me that it is not necessary and I didn't do that before. I start to explain how using the pillow started but she interrupts with, "That is an assumption." Another opportunity to surrender, so I simply say I won't use it next time. I don't and it works fine.

March 15, 1995

Last night seemed like a long night. We were up four times. I sometimes lose sight of the idea that I am serving Divine Mother when I am serving Swami Radha, as I get engrossed in concentrating on the details of what she needs. I try not to think too much. Just be there in the moment, ready for whatever is needed.

The last two times Swami Radha called me in the early morning I was in a deep sleep but also dreaming. My whole system feels jangled at having to leap up so suddenly and then be aware to lift her up completely straight and hold her there while she gets adjusted to sitting up. I am bending over and that seems to be hard on my back.

I feel tired and as soon as Julie and Arnon take over, I go to another room to sleep again. It is then I realize how jangled my nerves are. The strain of so much interrupted sleep must be having a cumulative effect. I feel better after a nap, but find myself close to tears. This tells me I am on the edge.

March 16, 1995

At 3:30 a.m. we watch a video about an investigation of the World Bank's financing of a huge dam project in India. It shows the effect on all the living beings, hundreds of thousands of people displaced and many species of birds and animals destroyed.

After the video is over, we go out to the swing and talk about it. I think she is trying to stimulate my thinking to look at the bigger picture. It takes me quite awhile to understand that she is talking about the evolution of human consciousness and that it is related to how people use energy.

She asks, "Why do you think those things happened to those people?"

I reply, "Well, at the very end of the show they briefly mentioned that some big sugar cane plantations were located below the dam and would benefit tremendously from the water supply. They were pushing it through." But she wants something more.

"But why were they successful in putting hundreds of thousands of people into a situation where they are dying of starvation? Why do you think these people's destiny allowed this to happen?"

I ponder this and say with uncertainty, "I don't know. It seems like mass karma."

She says, "Right." A long pause. "What other reason would there be?"

Another long pause while I search my mind for something more.

She is gentle but persistent. "You have heard me say it many times. I just want you to apply it now to your thinking."

Again I try to think what it would be, and suddenly it comes to me. "Well, does it have anything to do with evolution?"

"Yes! You have to cooperate with evolution or there are consequences. But I want to take it a little further. I think the Earth is here for a purpose – it's where we work out our karma. Many cultures have come and gone over time. Some traditions emphasize having children – the men's right to use women to produce baby after baby, and the neglect of the female, the mother aspect. There will come a time when Mother Earth will take revenge and correct matters. Overpopulation has to be controlled. That is partly the purpose of wars. People need to ask themselves, 'If I bring eight, nine, ten children into life, will they have a future?'

"The problem is the abuse of sexual energy, using it for pleasure instead of what it is for – procreation. Procreation has a minimal effect on the man. The major effect is on the woman and her way of life. Where you find attention paid to procreation and women more respected, things aren't so bad. If there were more discipline and family planning, the mortality rate for women and children would not be so high. Whenever family planning is raised, however, people bring up personal freedom. But there is no freedom without responsibility. That fact is totally ignored. Awareness and responsibility are dwindling so fast that it is quite obvious how the future is going to be.

"There are different catastrophes in each country. Even California has had its mudslides and fires. I want you to think about this in the world picture."

She brings up so much and puts it in a much bigger context. I wonder about the individuals who are cooperating with their evolution – how are they affected? But I see it is the use of Energy that is the important thing – how we use the vital life force; whether we use it for sexual gratification or to work toward our own evolution.

eighteen | BEING STRAIGHT

March 19, 1995 Spokane

This day is dedicated to celebrating Swami Radha's eighty-fourth birthday. We meet at the home of a devotee. People arrive from the Ashram,
and students from around the area have come, too – about fifty people
in all.

The room is set up with vases of roses around Swami Radha's
chair. People come in, bringing flowers, fruit or wrapped gifts. The
chanting begins as the room fills. When Swami Radha comes in, some
of us share our stories about how we met her. I tell the story of meeting
her in Virginia in 1967.

Then she talks and answers some questions. One of the swamis
says to her, "You have suffered a lot and you have achieved a lot. You
have set an example for all of us. What are your regrets?"

"I have no regrets," she says. "If somebody offers you a fake diamond from Woolworth's worth fifty cents and somebody else offers you
a real one, which would you choose? The power of choice is yours."

She talks about sacrifice and brings out a point I did not know,
although I knew she personally helped Jewish people escape Nazi Germany. "Most Canadians and Americans and the rest of the world don't
know that 60 000 Germans were exterminated because they helped

Jewish people. They were killed as traitors. But where the help is needed, you give it." I know that her husband, Wolfgang, was killed by the Gestapo for this reason.

"What is the purpose of your life? You are not here just to have fun. There is a course of evolution you can see everywhere. Learn through accepting the challenges. If you have done the best you could at the time, then there is nothing to regret."

She stops and looks down at the floor by her feet where people have placed their offerings. In a gentle voice she says, "I see some flowers on the floor. Will somebody please take care of them and give them some water?" There is something powerful in her simple words of awareness and caring.

March 20, 1995

Today is officially Swami Radha's birthday and the residents take her out for Spanish coffee. It turns into a family party. Swami Radha mentions the stories about meeting her that we told at her birthday celebration. She says they were not thought through and not specific enough. I feel myself reacting inside, but I tell my defensive aspect to step aside, and I listen so I can learn. She says it is not enough to say your life has been turned around. You have to explain how it was and what the changes are that have occurred. How are you different now from how you were before? Of course, this makes sense. But I thought I had done that. I need to reflect on what she has said so I can be clear.

April 1, 1995

It is afternoon and I have just come back from resting after a difficult morning. As I walk into the living room, Swami Radha smiles at me. "Arnon and I have been discussing options. She will go on night duty and you will sleep in the other bedroom and just be on call to help me in the bathroom. This will let you get a good sleep."

I can hardly believe what I am hearing. How did she know I was calling out to Divine Mother for help because of my recent back problems? My mind flips to this morning, how discouraged I felt when she got upset and said to me, "You used to know how to lift me up and use your body well but now you are doing it all wrong. I don't want to argue with you and spoil our relationship."

I wondered if I was not lifting her the same way. Was I doing something differently because I was unconsciously protecting my back? I know it is hard for her – living with constant pain is not easy. I didn't want to let her down or tell her about my back, but I was wondering how long I could keep going like this. I didn't know what to do, so when I went for my rest I turned to Divine Mother. "Please, Divine Mother, show me what to do. There must be a way."

After a walk in the fresh air I chanted in the prayer room, again asking Divine Mother for help. I remained receptive. And now the miracle happens. Swami Radha has tuned in to the Divine and knows what to do. I will move into the bedroom next to hers and answer her call only after Arnon gets her up. This will be very different, but it will give my back a rest. I am grateful for Swami Radha's perception. She has answered my call, a reversal of what I do, answering her call. Her ability to surrender completely allows that inner listening to happen.

Tonight I reflect on my body and how it has served me. I realize how I have taken for granted the miracle of my heart beating constantly for seventy years without a break. It doesn't tell me it needs a vacation or a tune-up or that it is tired of doing the same job. It just keeps going. It is like the muscles that expand the lungs and keep bringing in the breath that is necessary for my life. I don't have to think about it; it just happens. The entire working of my body is a miracle and I rarely stop to thank it or to really think about how miraculous all the various functions are. I still tend to push my body, although I am learning to give it the rest it needs. Swami Radha has shown me the way. She often says, "You are not the body, you are not the mind. You are Light Eternal." Keeping in touch with Divine Light gives me a different sense of the physical and brings more energy into the cells of my being. It works.

I am aware of how carefully she takes care of her physical body. She has told me that in the early days of the Ashram she pushed herself too hard, taking on all the responsibilities of getting it started. "I treated my body like a donkey. Don't do what I did. Treat your body like a temple, a Temple of Divine Light."

Doing the Divine Light Invocation regularly is a necessary part of my day. But I still have to do my part in cooperating with the Light.

April 16, 1995 Easter

We all go to a devotee's house for dinner, several cars full. After dessert we sing *bhajans*. We sing *Japo Ma* for Swami Radha, one of her favourites. She joins in by clapping her hands in time to the music. Afterward we gather around her expectantly and she talks to us. She starts with vibration.

"The human body has many vibrations. You can heal an area if you can find the right vibration for that part. Chant *Hari Om* and move the vibration around in your body. But you have to create a certain atmosphere first. Don't focus on the physical. Let's meet in the Light. This is also the way to build a bridge between the different cultures. We need to do this in these difficult times."

Another subject that comes up is jewelry.

"Sivananda bought jewelry after he made money as a medical doctor. Sometimes he put it all on at once. That was quite a display! But, of course, the symbolism was important. The necklace represents conquering self-will – total surrender to the Divine within."

Swami Radha closes the evening by asking us to chant. It is very peaceful with her there.

As we chant it comes to me that I was pursuing my approach to lifting her when getting her out of bed with the wrong focus – protecting my back. Perhaps the solution is to think of *embracing* her, thinking of her as Light and then she will be light. This way I can take it beyond the physical.

Later she talks to us about someone commenting that she is much too good to others. I mention her generosity, thoughtfulness and how much time she gives to people. She replies, "I think I have been too patient and this can mean less discipline." She gives examples of cracking down on a couple of students to enforce discipline; being too lenient leads to people being disrespectful. I feel she may be referring to me. I realize that when she came down so hard on me, I was forced to see many aspects of myself I didn't want to look at.

April 28, 1995

Often, I have been waking up just before Swami Radha awakes. Being with her so much must make me more attuned. Last night I had a dream:

I am dragging myself out of the dream, as I have to do something for Swami Radha. A part of me is holding on to the sleeping and dreaming, but another part is pulling me awake. It is important that I wake up. I look at the clock and it is midnight.

Within a few minutes I was called. Swami Radha really was getting up. It is all a strange experience.

How accepting she has to be of her limitations and the help she needs to go about her daily life. It must be hard to rely on people to tend to her most intimate needs and have them do the simplest things that she used to do easily for herself.

And there are so many disappointments. Today she receives a letter from two initiates, a couple who were with her for many years. They thanked her for all her help and guidance, but they were terminating their connection with her as disciples. It seems that people who I think are closely connected just leave, while others come in, sometimes in unexpected ways. It is like a river that flows through her life and whatever it brings or takes away has to be accepted. She has seen so much change. She takes it all as the Divine's plan.

April 29, 1995

"Be straight!"

Swami Radha corrects the way I lower her into her chair. She keeps telling me to be straight. I say I am straight. I feel annoyed. She doesn't understand the logistics. Lowering her down I bend my knees but I also have to come forward as well. Lifting her up I step back, which is easier. I don't think she understands this, as she keeps criticizing the way I do it. I guess I need to incorporate what she is telling me as much as possible and then let it go. Maybe it has to do with taking unjust criticism.

May 10, 1995

When Swami Radha calls for me the first time tonight I am super-careful with her, being as gentle as possible and checking with her. When we go to her desk she tells me to be straight as I lower her down to the chair. I say I thought I was straight.

Then I suddenly think of the other level of meaning. Perhaps she is using this situation to remind me to be straight in other areas of my life. She is waiting to see if I can get the message that there is more here than just my being physically straight. So I shift my attitude from a kind of defensive, self-righteous tone of voice to a lighter, surrendering one and I say, "Thank you for reminding me I am not straight. I need those reminders." Knowing the Guru is there to help remind me creates a very different feeling inside. I can let go of the defensiveness and not harbour negative emotions. This is a necessary aspect of surrender. But I also know that I need to reflect on where I am not straight in my life.

I have not been straight with her by trying to solve my back problem without telling her. This is a dilemma because I don't want to make an issue of it when she has enough to deal with. Is this just an excuse?

I think she knows I have understood because the next time I lower her into the chair she looks at me with a twinkle in her eye and we both laugh. Now I feel her welcoming me in, whereas before I felt cut off from her. Is this all because of my shift in attitude? Was the previous feeling of being shut out just created by my own uncultivated imagination? It is so hard to get at the facts and the underlying truth of a situation when the mind goes around and around building its own story.

I think of the Tibetan yogi, Milarepa, who took his guru's criticism and just kept doing what was asked even when it seemed completely illogical. Instead of thinking it wasn't worth all the hard work, harbouring resentment, and being critical of his guru, he just kept moving the huge pile of rocks from one place to another. This was how Milarepa's guru helped him to polish his inner diamond. So staying with it, no matter what, is important. It is meeting the challenges that brings the treasure. The pearl of great price is worth the price.

Putting myself in Swami Radha's place, I see how she is risking that I will get disgusted and turn away or think it is not worth the hassle. In terms of conventional life it may not seem to make sense, but I have to take this in a much larger perspective.

One thing that emerges is my lack of confidence in myself. In some areas I have built more confidence, but in others I am unsure whether decisions that I make are appropriate. I still seem to be fearful of doing something wrong. Yet the other side of the coin is a tendency to plunge ahead impulsively, not communicating with others about it. Then I want to make decisions on my own, do my own thing. I don't want to have to deal with people. Do I fear their criticism or that they won't understand my point of view? The two sides of the coin may be more related than I thought.

It takes careful awareness to be able to see what I am doing and what my motivation is. Swami Radha is trying to help me get stronger and clearer in myself. This is her job. My ego wants to justify its position and to maintain the status quo. I have to be willing to extract the learning from each situation and apply it to show I am indeed learning.

nineteen | BETWEEN DARK & LIGHT

May 16, 1995 Spokane

I sit with Swami Radha in the morning and do some sewing for her while she is sleeping. Later I do my mantra practice. The mantra seems very haunting and I chant quietly. An image appears. It looks like Krishna ahead of me, reaching back toward me and smiling as if to encourage me to come. It is dark, almost like a tunnel, but there is light beyond so we are moving toward the Light. It seems like the descriptions of a near death experience.

May 22, 1995

Swami Radha told me she had a dream about me. "You are gathering lots of brown and white eggs. You say we should sort out the white ones as we can sell them for more money to a restaurant. What do you make of that, Egg Lady?" She looked at me and started to laugh. I joined in and told her I didn't know I was doing that.

Tonight, I was in a very deep sleep and had to be called twice. I have been tired. Swami Radha asks me, "Why is your door shut, what is the secret?"

I tell her, "It is because my window is open and the air is cool. I don't want the cool air to go into the hall to bother you."

"It is dangerous to have your window open," she responds. "Some-one could break in."

I say, "Oh, it is very unlikely as they would need a ladder and I would hear them. I don't think we need to be concerned about that."

There is a pause and then out of the blue she says, "Well, you could put some boxes of eggs under the window and he would step on them and crack them. That would wake us up!" Then she bursts into laughter that makes me laugh as well. She laughs until her eyes are brimming with tears and I feel myself getting lighter and lighter with laughter. Later she tells everyone about it, continuing to get a laugh from it.

May 26, 1995

I wake up twice in the night just before Swami Radha calls. The last time she says to me, "I think of you now as the Egg Lady. It is good that my unconscious sees you as someone who is looking out for my well-being and wants to help." I feel the warmth in her voice and am happy to be the Egg Lady.

June 1, 1995

This evening Swami Radha has a guest, so I stay in my room and read a book on Egypt that a friend has sent me. I read a part about Thoth, whose symbol is the moon. "...the moon becomes a more challenging symbol, for it must work in the darkness, symbolic of the realm of the lost ones." I am not one of the lost ones!

I feel a heaviness and fall asleep as I'm reading this part. When I wake up I decide just to go to bed and for the first time, I do not do the Light Invocation or any reflections. I just turn the light out. It is around 11 o'clock.

I must have gone into a dream soon after:

I am in a house with my mother and father. I am in a room by myself.

It is very dark. There is a presence in the room and I don't know what it is. I have fallen onto the floor on the left side of the bed. I see a shadowy figure, very large, moving to the right in front of me. I call for help but it is hard for me to make any sound. I don't think my mother or father will hear, but I keep calling, "Help!" I feel very alone in the dark, in the unknown.

Arnon awakens me, opening the door and asking if I am all right. I have been calling out loud for help. I tell her I have been dreaming of a dark room and a presence that I can't see. It is 11:20 so I wasn't asleep very long.

I wonder if I am contacting a dark part of me that I have been afraid to look at. Or did my reading about Egypt bring back a memory of something fearful that happened in a previous lifetime? Did the fact that I hadn't done the Light Invocation mean that I was not protected? It is a strange dream experience. I do not recall crying out like that in my sleep for a very long time.

I do the Divine Light Invocation immediately and get my initiation *mala* to hold. I hold it all night. Arnon tells me later that I had called out like someone in deep distress. She says she wrote up the incident herself as a waking dream experience for her own reflections.

June 3, 1995

Swami Radha offers some clarification about the nightmare I had. Immediately she says to take off the scarab necklace she gave me recently. She says it takes awhile for the energy on jewelry to neutralize. She didn't say whether or not this might have had an influence on the dream. But she adds, "You don't reflect enough. You have to think more about what these things mean. It takes constant awareness."

Then she tells me, "When I am watching television you can work on dreams or your own reflections. You can sit in the kitchen or on the swing so you can hear me when I call. This is to be distinguished from when I am talking with someone or being read aloud to because then you can sit and listen.

"You need to develop your intuitive perceptions better. Instead of asking how I am feeling, see if you can tell from a place of inner knowing. Be aware of your speech and observe if you are being mechanical."

I try to remember all of this as she continues. "I'm tired of telling people not to wear secondhand clothes where they take on the vibrations of other people. Things have to be neutralized and this takes a long time." When I mention this to two other residents later they both say she has never mentioned it to them, although she knows they both wear secondhand clothes. So she must be making a point with me and I need to reflect on it.

Wearing other people's clothes means picking up their vibrations, their emotions, their highs and lows. Clothes are the image one presents to the world. If I wear other people's clothes, I present a mixed image. How do I present a mixed image? When I am not clear in myself, when I take on other people's ideas, when I identify with other people's problems, when I seek variety in my life. Swami Radha has also mentioned that I have to know how much of a reminder of *sanyas* I need in terms of orange clothes.[1]

The message here is to be very aware of when I am drawn outward to distractions or new and exciting things. Also, as a protection, I am doing the Divine Light Invocation more. I focus on Swami Radha and me together in the Light. It is really important to truly listen to her. Perhaps she is giving me a harsh message outwardly and a different message mentally. I have to listen to the inner level to pick that up. After she talked sternly to me this morning there was a bit of a twinkle and a smile. I smiled back just to show her I understood.

June 10, 1995

Swami Radha speaks to me about women being more powerful than men. "You know, Durgananda, at one time woman may have been able to reproduce herself, but could only reproduce the feminine." My

---

1 Orange (or saffron) is the traditional colour worn by *sanyasins*. Swami Radha added blue as a second colour for the renunciates of her line.

understanding is that all fetuses start out with feminine characteristics and the masculine is only added later, so this idea makes sense.

Then she mentions my slow development. "Progress is slow in the beginning, until you wake up, and then it is fast. That is why I am trying to make you wake up! I hope you live another ten years because it will take you that long. You have to keep putting in the effort."

I feel discouraged after this. Will I ever make it? How do I wake up? Why does it happen to some people who don't even try? I try to do right action, balancing the practices with Karma Yoga and doing what I am asked to do. Does this mean nothing? Swami Radha would say that it doesn't mean that nothing has been done, just that it won't get me there, that it is not enough.

But I don't want to be caught in the negative. When I look at my victories I recognize the other side. I have made progress. I am much stronger in myself and I am becoming more clear as I learn each day from Swami Radha. My reflections on the challenges I experienced are taking me deeper, my concepts are being overturned. My growing understanding of surrender is helping me care for Swami Radha.

The spiritual path is not an easy path. It is a constant challenge. I have made a commitment that has its own force that pulls me along. But I still have to do the work.

June 17, 1995

This afternoon we talk a little about past lives. She says it is not good to be drawn into the past. "You wouldn't want to go back and play with the teddy bear you had as a three-year-old." She also says nostalgia may draw me back and that is an obstacle. I think nostalgia would be more in the past in this life than in a former life. She tells me to watch my dreams and they will tell me what I need to know. "Don't investigate or try to discover something."

This sounds different from what she has said previously, as she seemed to be encouraging me to find out about my Egyptian life. I don't particularly want to find out, but she keeps giving me Egyptian things. That seems to give the message that I should try to recall. I am happy to wait and allow whatever is necessary to come up. That way, it will be only what I can handle, especially if it is negative.

I ask her about the idea of inception and what it means. She clarifies, "What is before inception? First, there is the departure of your vortex of Energy and consciousness from the life before. Then there is a decision of where you will be born and to whom. This is your responsibility. But it may be where you would learn the most: to be a devotee of selfless service."

She told me once that when you get in touch with a past life it gives you a different sense of time. Sivananda knew about their past lives together but she didn't. Whenever she asked him about this he changed the subject.

June 24, 1995

A bear is loose in the street where I lived when I was very young. It has run off in the distance and then turns and comes back toward me. I have no fear because I know that all I have to do is stand still and stare intently at it. I am holding a staff in my hand. As the bear comes closer I raise the staff and stand as tall as I can and stare at it with all the power I have. The bear slows down, then looks down at the ground and walks respectfully around me, giving me a wide distance and then keeps going. I have a feeling of power. I really feel like Durga.

I have had bears in my dreams before. Bears are associated with the goddess in Greek mythology. I tend to project my fear onto them. They can be fierce, though from a distance they seem mild. However, they can be unpredictable and very protective of their young. In this sense they are symbolic of anger. Instinctual nature has a lot of energy and power. In me this needs to be channeled and controlled so it doesn't get scattered or misused.

I feel as if Durga is showing her strength. The "I" in the dream is powerful and strong. The staff is a power symbol like the staff of Moses, the staff of life, the spine.

This dream shows me I have made a lot of progress since my previous bear dreams where the bears were often chasing me and I tried to hide from them. I am sure my time with Swami Radha is helping me get stronger in myself.

This morning Swami Radha goes through some old photographs and finds one of Sivananda holding her finger and guiding her to form the Durga yantra on some sand. He was giving her some kind of Durga initiation. "So it makes sense that I would have a Durgananda for a disciple," she says.

June 30, 1995

When I get up with Swami Radha at 5:20 a.m. she asks, "Is it time for Durgananda coffee?" I reply, "Anytime is a good time." Then she tells me, "No, that is all right; go back to bed and have a good dream."

But I don't feel right about leaving her, so I make coffee. She is pleased and says, "Well, there is one medication that really works for me and that is Durgananda coffee."

July 8, 1995

Tonight Swami Radha meets with several of us. She is straight and direct.

"Make a list of the spiritual practices you have done and for how long. Any results? If not, why not?"

Later the question arises: What is meant by results? I get the impression that we are supposed to have certain specific results and if we don't have those results, then we have missed the boat. I experience the effect of the practices in my life in various ways that are meaningful to me, but may not be what is expected. Over a period of time, after I have been doing the Divine Light Invocation for someone or for a relationship, I notice a change happening, as if the Light has an effect that is more subtle than a dramatic experience. This happened when I put my marriage relationship in the Light. My own feelings

changed and my former husband became more mellow and understanding.

July 27, 1995

I answer Swami Radha's call in the night. I feel half asleep as I meet her
and Arnon outside my door. She holds onto my wrists to start walking
and says, "I should have you go into my bed to warm it up for me. You
are like a hot water bottle with ears." We both laugh.

This afternoon chanting in the prayer room there is joy, sunshine,
colour, song; Krishna calling; the Goddess calling; Durga beckoning.
I think about a suggestion Swami Radha has made to reflect on the
kingdom of God: it is within. It is all within me. I don't need to go
anywhere, be anywhere else. Turn within and dive deep into my inner
self. This has nothing to do with my physical form. My essence lives on
even when my physical self drops away.

The kingdom of God reflects the essence. It is always there, but
I can choose to be in a mind state that is the opposite, an inner hell.
The Divine takes me to a place of awareness in my own inner Self. My
Divine nature is there. It draws my consciousness to it, to the kingdom.
I join the kingdom, become one with it. There is no longer a sense of
separation. I am it.

July 28, 1995

A week ago, early in the night, the image came into my mind of a *mala*
made of alternating wooden, jade and pearl beads. I was not sure if
I was asleep or dreaming, or in a state between waking and sleeping.
Today I receive a sandalwood *mala* that I ordered from the Ashram
bookstore so that I can follow through on this dream. I thread this
new *mala* with some old jade beads from a necklace a friend once gave
me and pearls from a bracelet that my uncle gave me a long time ago,
together with the wooden beads, in a repeating pattern that comes to
108, which is a sacred number. Divine Mother has 108 names.

August 11, 1995

Swami Radha and I watch a video of the Dalai Lama. I am impressed with the similarity between what he says and what she teaches. He talks about renunciation, what effect the Light has on someone who really practises it, how real meditation is much more than just closing one's eyes. The goal of self-realization is not reached without effort and time.

I tell her about my *mala* dream and show her the finished *mala*. She sees it as my separating things, as the many things I do. But she also says it is the most unusual *mala* she has ever seen. I am going to stay with my feeling about it and use it to help my focus as the three kinds of beads all have a different feel, which holds my attention better.

August 14, 1995

I give Swami Radha a massage this morning. She seems able to bear more pressure now and she feels it is helping her circulation and stimulating her muscles.

Later she tells me I was the most focused and absorbed when I was doing the illustrations for the Hidden Language book. I remember she gave me the assignment and set things up so it was my only focus. Now it seems I am given a number of suggestions of things to do. Do I prioritize her suggestions, or do I just choose one or two? Why does she suggest things if she doesn't want me to follow through? Is she just testing me? Tempting me? Or does she forget that she has made a number of suggestions? What is right action?

All of a sudden she decides she wants to take me shopping for clothes – right now! So a couple of us rush around getting everything together. We go to a department store and I find a beautiful dress on sale. We all like it, so I buy it. Then we go to another store and Swami Radha finds a stunning evening dress in a wine colour with embroidery on the jacket. It looks very elegant and she wants to buy it for me. I am to wear it when I give lectures. It gives me a look of dignity and that is the way she wants me to look.

I say it is very special and she says, "Well, you are special. You are about 90 percent special and only 10 percent criticism." And then she adds, "And that's not bad at all." She takes us out to lunch afterward and when I offer to pay she says no, that I have to be humble.

August 24, 1995

My days with Swami Radha are very full. I am up by 6:30 a.m. to be with her. Then the morning is taken up with things related to her care or the apartment. I have kept my mantra practice going. The amount of time I can give to it doesn't seem to matter. It is the sweetness of the experience that matters.

I have been interested in Swami Radha's training of Arnon. She has told Arnon to stay up all night and do practices when she is not up with her. A couple of mornings ago when I got up to relieve her, Swami Radha suggested watching the video of the dialogue between the Benedictine monks and the Dalai Lama. When Arnon suggested she could watch it later, as she was tired, Swami Radha talked to her intensely about letting go of concepts about sleep and sacrificing the need for sleep. So Arnon stayed and watched it, and even made the decision to forego her usual nap.

Afterward we talked about Jesus being quoted in the video as telling his disciples that if they are not accepted in certain villages, they should shake the dust from their feet and move on. The Dalai Lama laughed and said it showed some resentment that Jesus had. Swami Radha said it means not to waste time with those who are not receptive. I suggested it means to shake off the negativity and leave it behind so they don't take it with them. All three comments seem valid.

After supper I am in the room where I sleep, sitting on the bed reading and leaning against the wall. Swami Radha peers around the corner and questions me about my position. "Durgananda, remember about your spine. It is where the energy moves; if you are always spine-conscious, you keep the body straight. Then this works on the unconscious and you become straight in your life. Sit straight instead of slouching. This develops honesty."

"Thanks, Swami Radha, I need that reminder again." I move to sit on the floor on a pillow with my spine supported straight against the bed.

twenty | THE CALL

August 26, 1995 Spokane

When I am helping Swami Radha dress after her massage, she says, "Arnon told me that I called you when we were still in the living room walking toward the hall, and yet you heard me and responded instantly. So you must be tuned into me." What a relief! Perhaps I truly am making progress. She continues, "I see you are using your energy better. You are conserving it and you are being gentle when you can. This saves it up for when you need it."

I think about listening and about the call I receive, waking me so many times from a deep sleep state, calling me to awareness and to the service of my Guru, my name being called. Sometimes it is her call, gentle yet clear and direct. I hear it right away. Sometimes it is Arnon's voice – a softer call, but I still hear it. I am listening for it in one part of my mind. This afternoon as I chant I try calling my name quietly and hear the power of that sound, that vibration.

Another part of the listening process was sleeping at the foot of her bed for two months, hearing her breathing, listening for her call. Then sleeping in the room next to her with only a thin wall between us. I think of the time I was with her in the hospital when she moved through the crisis, sometimes being in the room with her all night and responding to her needs. Each one of these opportunities brought me closer to her, helping me learn the lessons of surrender, forming a closer bond between us. I have a deep sense of gratitude. I am doing what I am called to do, and I accept the privilege of being called to serve. Nothing else matters.

August 27, 1995

While Swami Radha sleeps this morning I do some Hatha quietly. In the sitting forward bend, as I stretch up, bend forward, and lay my upper body over my legs, I think about laying my life down and putting it at the feet of the Divine. Putting my life on the line: this is the essence of surrender to the Divine. I am aware of the release coming slowly, a little at a time. Surrender happens in this way, as well, at least in my experience. It is a step-by-step letting-go. I go further each time. I feel I have done this with Swami Radha, and she gives me the chance over and over to go beyond what I think are my limitations.

I feel the letting-go as a natural expression of my vow of *sanyas*. I am acting from strength and a sense of grace. I even have a feeling of adventure, moving into a new attitude or action that may be entering unknown territory. I welcome it and am grateful.

The main development over the last few days is planning for a group initiation that Swami Radha will give at a devotee's house near Spokane in Hayden Lake on September 8th. This has all come about because of a pearl ring one of the residents gave her recently. It is very unusual, with a large cluster of freshwater pearls, each pierced and anchored to a gold ring. Swami Radha has kept the ring on her desk, often looking at it carefully. She tells us it suggests to her the symbol of many seekers all grounded in the gold of the teachings; this gave her the message to offer a mantra pronouncement open to everyone, as she saw her Guru do soon after she arrived in India in 1954. Swami Radha's feeling is that those who are serious will take the mantra to heart and do something with it.

She wants to tell the story of the pearl ring on video and she invites us for a video session in the evening. She tells me to wear the new evening gown she gave me. She is in top form, very charming and lively. I think about the devotee, the messenger who gave her this special ring. Will she take it into her heart and really accept her role and the significance of what it means? It is such an important symbol.

August 29, 1995

The excitement is mounting for the big day on September 8th. It is like a wave that ripples out from a central force and affects people in all directions. People have to face their commitment and priorities. Some say they are coming no matter what and others say they have a prior engagement or they have a money problem. The power of choice lies with each individual. Swami Radha is not choosing; she is opening a door for all who choose to come through.

Yesterday, Swami Radha asked me to call an old friend of hers to tell her about the mantra pronouncement. The friend was almost in tears, she was so touched. She said she would do anything she could to be there in spite of her arthritis. But today, Swami Radha said to me, "Call her back and tell her she does not need to come. Tell her to tune in between 2:00 and 4:00 in the afternoon on September 8th and Swami Radha will meet her in the Light. Then perhaps she can come here for a visit later when she is feeling better." I go right to the phone and call her. She is overwhelmed with gratitude.

August 30, 1995

I think about the purpose of my time here with Swami Radha. She has talked often about preparing myself for the transition to the other side and the importance of a focus on my practices. She has mentioned that it is necessary to establish a close connection with her now, so there can be a connection in spirit with her when she is no longer here physically.

I have been given the gift of close contact with her, so that I can be aware of what she needs without words being said. When I walk backward with her, I rely on her guidance, the subtle pressure she makes with her hands on my wrists or a slight turn of the body. I am feeling my way rather than seeing my way, trusting her and surrendering to her guidance. This is certainly a way of developing a connection on another level.

September 1, 1995

Swami Radha suggested awhile ago that I reflect on why I chose a woman guru. It is an auspicious time to reflect now before the mantra pronouncement. In one sense, I didn't actually choose her but seemed to be guided to her. It must have been a past life connection that drew me to her. But beyond that, it is obvious that a woman guru knows the needs of a woman much more clearly, from the heart level. She knows what women have been through, as she has experienced the situations, the conditions, the feelings, the longing that other women have. She knows the traps, the conditioning and the weaknesses that I as a woman have accepted as part of myself. She knows about financial and emotional dependence on the male. She knows the hidden longing for spiritual fulfillment, the empty vessel waiting to be filled.

She has experienced the rejections and put-downs that most women receive, but as a guru she also knows the way out. She knows there is a great potential in women. I have to accept that in myself as well, including endurance, patience and enormous creativity waiting to be released and used. She knows how to bring out the best in me and she helped me out of the ditch as she has so many other women. Right from the beginning I valued her down-to-earth, practical approach to spiritual life. I appreciated her emphasis on bringing quality into all that I do, and how she let me find my way with her guidance when I got off track. But she let me make my own discoveries.

I also feel that I can trust her. As I got to know her, I saw her greatness of character. I knew she would not take advantage of me. I was shocked by the scandals that many gurus were involved in, taking advantage of their disciples sexually and financially.

Her devotional side is deep and she has a sharp mind. As a female guru she has a natural opening of the heart fueled by compassion. Maybe this has something to do with the unconditional love mothers feel for their children. She often says unconditional love has no "because." She has brought out that devotional quality in her disciples, men and women, showing us all ways to develop our heart connection to the Divine. In her it is strong. She is the way to connect with Divine Mother; she is the link. She expresses the qualities of Divine Mother: compassion, patience, acceptance, gentleness. But she also has the fire, the ability to prod and cut through that is necessary to take action and make changes. The mother is the link to the father and the woman guru is the mother. Swami Radha leads me to the Divine Father. But I turn to the Mother for understanding, help and compassion. She shows me the way to self-realization.

September 7, 1995

We had such a good time last night when Swami Radha invited everyone to her apartment. We celebrated with a couple who had a spiritual marriage ritual. We played a tape of some lively dance music from an Indian film. Swami Radha told us all to dance and we had such fun laughing and dancing around, bumping into each other in the crowded space. Swami Radha looked on from her chair, clapping and smiling. Afterward, we had cheesecake as *prasad*.

And now a full day preparing for the mantra pronouncement tomorrow. Yet I do not feel pressured. In the evening we help with the preparations there – arranging flowers, setting up chairs, and hanging pictures of Swami Radha and Swami Sivananda in India. These are placed carefully on the wall behind Swami Radha's chair.

I get acquainted with the video camera. I will be holding it steadily on Swami Radha while another camera person will move around getting other shots. We manage to fit about 140 chairs into the room. It is hard to know how it will work out, but people are coming and Swami Radha is doing quite well.

September 8, 1995 The Mantra Pronouncement

My spiritual birthday is today. It has been eleven years since my mantra initiation and six years since my *sanyas* initiation. So much I have been given. Now I am trying to give back the best I can. Right now as I sit with Swami Radha while she sleeps, I focus on the Light. It is important for me to support her on this day as she brings the mantra to many devotees. She needs all the support possible.

It is a perfect day – clear and not too hot. I help Swami Radha get dressed and then she tells me to go out to Hayden Lake early so I can get set up for the video work.

As soon as I arrive I go to the guestroom, which is filling up with Ashram and Radha House women, chatting and putting on white saris and Punjabi outfits. I help a few of them and then go down to tend the camera. Chanting starts around one o'clock as people are arriving, coming from all over, coming together for this once-in-a-lifetime occasion. Excitement and anticipation fill the air as they settle into their seats and join the chanting. Before long the chairs are all filled. Gradually the atmosphere changes and a feeling of reverence fills the room.

Swami Radhananda starts by welcoming everyone. Another swami gives a talk on initiation and what it means. She explains what the mantra pronouncement is, so people know what to expect. Those who take the mantra to the heart will have the benefits.

Swami Radha enters with Julie and settles into her chair. There is more chanting and I see that Swami Radha's eyes are closed. When we stop chanting there is silence and she explains in a sentence what Hari represents and what Om means. Then she pronounces the mantra once very firmly and clearly – *Hari Om.*

We chant *Hari Om* as people start to come up two at a time to offer their flowers and gifts and have their *malas* blessed. I am really touched at how Swami Radha gives each person attention, taking each *mala,* wrapping it around her hand and repeating the mantra silently on several beads. With some she puts the *mala* back over the person's head. Several people give her a rosary and she tells them they may chant Jesus Christ to the *Hari Om* melody. With a few, she gives an extra pat on their hand as she gives the *mala* back. Toward the end when one devotee hands her a wooden flute she is delighted.

I can see what an effort it is for her to be constantly reaching out for what people are offering her. And when she hands back the *mala* some people refrain from reaching forward enough to help her. This means she has to strain to stretch her arm out further. I wonder why they are not aware of being considerate of her. She goes on for two hours; then finally turns to Julie to say she needs a rest. While she is gone everyone has a stretch and we do the Divine Light Invocation for her. When she returns she is as perky and full of Light as when she started. It is remarkable how she is able to keep giving.

She concludes with a few minutes of silence in which people are asked to feel the vibration of the mantra in their bodies and their hearts. She says to leave in silence and keep the mantra going.

After everyone has left several of us go up on the porch where Swami Radha is having a bite to eat. She looks out over the lake, which is perfectly still and peaceful, with lovely reflections on it. She seems fine and takes her time before getting ready to return to her apartment.

I am amazed at how Swami Radha kept going for the whole time. She was obviously being given the energy she needed. It shows me the power of surrender and what the years of practice can do. I am grateful to have been a part of this experience. I wonder what effect it will have on the people who participated.

twenty-one | THE CHARIOT COMES

September 26, 1995 Yasodhara Ashram

In the evening I represent the Ashram at a community meeting about "The Spiritual Dimension of Death and Dying." The purpose is to bring ideas to caregivers and hospice volunteers. I didn't know what to expect and am surprised to see so many people. We sit in a circle and I am relieved to see that I know the chairperson and a few of the other people involved.

The speakers represent different faiths in the local community. One person quotes the Bible and talks about faith. The next one reads from a book on near-death experiences that tell about unpleasant experiences like hell. His approach is that you have to accept Jesus in order to be saved. Another person reads about five pages of what his sect believes.

I know the priest representing the Catholic Church. He comes right from the heart. He speaks of how he has been given much by those who died when he was with them. He tells about a woman dying of cancer who asked him to do the Divine Light Invocation with her as she was lying in bed. He had learned this from the Ashram and was glad to be able to help her in this way. He said how important it is to just sit with the dying in the Light. His words are touchingly real.

I speak last and talk about the tools that yoga gives us to help us prepare for our own death and to help others. I mention the corpse pose and the importance of relaxing. This is helpful for the dying patient as well as the caregiver. I say that dreams also may help prepare the dying person. Finally, I explain the Divine Light Invocation as a way to connect with the Light that dying people often experience. The caregiver can also use the Light as a tool to help release the patient from pain or fear.

I am asked to teach the Divine Light Invocation. I feel concerned about people present who may not be open to it, so I say I am willing to teach those who are interested. The chairperson suggests that those who wish to learn it participate and those who don't remain seated. I demonstrate and lead them through the practice. Afterward, several people tell me they appreciated my presentation because I gave practical ways of helping. It's rewarding to use the teachings as a tool for those in need.

September 29, 1995 Spokane

I join Swami Radha to watch Puccini's *Turandot*. I have not seen the first two acts, so I am glad to have the opportunity. I do not stay for the third act, as I have seen that one so often that the music gets into my mind and overrides the mantra. It is interesting that one theme in both *Turandot* and *Lohengrin* has to do with the name of the hero being revealed. Each comes from royalty or a tradition representing a Divine purpose that is not to be revealed to the masses. There was a reason in each case. Are we meant to keep our Divine heritage in our hearts and not reveal it?

October 1, 1995

A very difficult situation comes up today. One of the swamis arrives to see Swami Radha and to tell her she is leaving. I feel sad that she has rejected her *sanyas* vows and her commitment. It feels like a kind of death to me. Perhaps this is on my mind after being at the hospice meeting. I am sure Swami Radha will keep the door open for her, as she has done for others who have left. But they can't come back on their own terms. And once the vows are renounced that part is over.

I wonder why this is happening to Swami Radha at this time in her life. Yet when she hears about it she seems much less upset than I am. She comments that at least this woman was courageous enough to make the attempt at *sanyas*. Later she calls the Ashram to inform them what has happened. She tells Swami Radhananda to assist the woman if she asks for help when she comes to pick up her things.

October 4, 1995

When Swami Radha gets up this morning we go over to her desk. I kneel at her feet while she talks to me about commitment for the *sanyasin*. She says it is a very different thing from any commitment made by a person who has not taken *sanyas*.

I tell her, "I have tried not to let this recent situation pull me down. I want to keep the Light as my focus, but it is hard. She and I had many years as friends and *gurubais*.[1] I would think you would get discouraged when this happens." She looks at me very straight and says, "The Divine gives and the Divine takes away, and we don't know what the next step will be."

Then her tone changes as she sits back in her chair. "Because of the karmic repercussions it is necessary to stay with your vows. At first I thought the Indians exaggerated when they talked about this, but then I found that the Cayce readings confirmed it. He said people who misuse the Divine intelligence in one lifetime have to come back without that intelligence the next time." She looks at me very intently and compassionately and says, "When the time for transition comes, you will find out that it was all worth it." Then she leans forward and embraces me. I feel her love pouring into me and I am close to tears as I sense the depth of our connection.

---

1   *Gurubais* are people who have been initiated by the same guru.

October 11, 1995

In the night Swami Radha is in a high mood and very funny when we get up around 2:00 a.m. She says something about Durgananda dancing to the bathroom. Then she says, "Or is it the Egg Lady?" She is so impish I begin to laugh and she mimics me as if I am dancing. Arnon says later that she mentioned my name in her sleep so I must have been on her mind. I never know what is going to happen next!

As we walk, she again calls me her "hot water bottle with ears." She says that is what she used to call her husband, Wolfgang, because he was so warm that she would get him to heat up the bed for her.

October 14, 1995

I stay with Swami Radha during the day. We read and watch videos. While she is engrossed in reading, she suggests I get my book and read, so there we are, on each side of her desk, quietly reading. I think she likes that kind of stillness. I like it, too, just being with her, immersed in my own focus. Being with her in the daytime again is an experience of awareness and caring, making sure I ask her what she wants and trying to be attentive and considerate.

Before supper Swami Radha inspects the new wheelchair ramp outside. Everyone gathers as she gives her approval. Oddly, she turns to the subject of discipline and mentions that she has never believed in breaking someone's spirit. She says she learned from how elephants are trained. The driver has to break the elephant's spirit to get it to obey, and she compares that to some monasteries where often the spirit is broken.

She points out a very different way. "It is most important that you have a love affair with the Divine."

October 19, 1995

Tonight Arnon and I discuss the action the guru has to take to help a disciple. There is a difference between an ordinary person lashing out in anger and the guru getting angry to wake up a disciple. I think of the dream I had before I came to the Ashram about having an appointment with Swami Radha and she slaps my face. I knew it was to wake me up. Swami Radha never actually slaps people, of course, but my knowing part presented her this way to emphasize how important it is for me to wake up.

October 25, 1995

Oh, negative destructive voices rushing in, trying to overpower me. What is going on with me lately? The buffalo-headed demon and his army are coming to face me. I sleep until after seven o'clock this morning and should feel well rested, but I am so stiff I can hardly get up. Last night I was up five times in six hours. My body is longing for a consistent rest. Resistance sets in. How am I going to get through today? How do I shift my attitude? If I allow the negative to take over, I am not doing selfless service.

When Yasoda tells me Swami Radha is ready to have her hair brushed, I can't believe that I snap back, "I'm not ready." I do the Divine Light Invocation to shift my negative reaction. I must get this under control; I don't want to project anything onto Swami Radha. Once I start working with her hair, a calmness comes over me. But as I help her to get dressed another lesson arises about assumptions.

She asks me to get her pink sweater. I always feel that trying to find exactly what she wants is a test. I look in the drawers where her sweaters are kept, but can't find it. She says impatiently that she is sure it is there and goes with me to look again. In the bottom drawer she picks up a white sweater she hasn't worn in ages. I assumed the pink sweater would not be under it, but it is. She gives me a stern look and I silently remind myself yet again: Look more carefully. Don't make assumptions. How many times have I said this!

I want to put all of my heart into serving Swami Radha. This is my practice. I need to keep it pure, not tainted with selfishness or ego. It is in the little daily details that I have the opportunity to learn so much about awareness and surrender.

October 26, 1995

I rake leaves this afternoon, and then do my mantra practice with re-flection. It helps to start with prayer dance because this shifts my fo-cus to the Divine immediately. During chanting I seem to be drawn to an abstract sense of the Divine, not wanting to give it form. This takes me more into the feeling level, strangely enough. No image to focus on, so I move more to the feeling, to the heart, to make a con-nection.

It is amazing that after the challenges of yesterday I have such a different experience today. I use my time efficiently and it expands, giving me space to do more.

October 29, 1995

At supper I observe myself sinking into an old place, feeling annoyed and not communicating because of a difficult situation. I shut myself off by doing this and I don't like it. In the past when this happened, I would feel ignored, left out, hurt, not appreciated – all ego-related. But now I understand more about bringing unresolved situations forward so they don't smoulder. In my mantra practice I am able to see the situ-ation in a proper perspective, but the residue of emotions still hangs around the edges. I will have to talk to the person involved or there will be an undercurrent. If I present my feelings and suggest options, I will not be projecting blame onto her. This makes such a difference. I wish I had known this in my early years.

November 14, 1995

Early in the night, I dream:
A figure is standing by my bed. I awake and say, "Oh, is it time to get up?" I am sure I am being called. I have the feeling that the figure has power and protection associated with it. There is a sense of being taken care of and being given strength. The word angel comes to me.

Then the door opens and Arnon calls my name – it is time to get up. The image and the feeling stay with me the rest of the night and I awake feeling rested.

November 16, 1995

I am walking along a street looking at the backs of houses trying to identify them. I see a pink house with a For Sale sign on it and realize that it is the Pink Lady's house.

The pink house is next door. The woman in it seems to live in fantasy and illusions. We call her the Pink Lady. She is an older woman trying to look and act young, but she has to face these illusions now and sell the house because she can no longer manage to live alone.

The pink house is for sale. Pink is a colour usually associated with little girls, a cultural view of the feminine. If these are parts of me, then I am encouraged that I am getting rid of them. I am letting go of illusions that hold me back.

Pink Lady illusions have to do with youth, romance and marriage. I had illusions about my marriage, wanting it to have the harmony of my parents' marriage. Since I am not in a marriage now I have to look at other kinds of relationships. I have two important ones: with the Divine and with Swami Radha. Both have commitments, vows and certain expectations.

Illusions about the Divine: I need some sign, an experience, something concrete to let me know that I am on the right track, doing all right. I think I can't keep my passion alive without this constant reassurance. But signs have been given to me that I did not even recognize. I have received guidance and protection and some very concrete signs. The Divine is mysterious, mostly intangible, can't be grasped, seen or touched. The Divine needs to be perceived in other ways, sometimes very subtle ways. Illusions have no solidity or foundation. Stay with my trust, faith, commitment, and what I learned from the past. Remain true and open.

Sometimes I have the illusion that Swami Radha is all Radha without accepting the human parts. I am seeing the reality and the value of the integration of those parts more and more. Each serves a purpose. I have to be careful of having unrealistic expectations of her as a guru. That is an unfair burden to put on her.

Illusions from my past. Selfishness. I always thought of my husband as selfish, but I was selfish also, focused on my problems, on my situation, on my feelings. Both of us had much growing up to do. This old pattern of focusing on myself surfaces in the struggle I have at times in taking care of Swami Radha. But I am catching it more now.

Another is neediness. My neediness arises now by focusing on the wrong thing, thinking I need something for my well-being.

All these attitudes connect. If I work on one, it helps eliminate the others.

November 23, 1995

American Thanksgiving. We gather in the prayer room, where a lively discussion develops. Swami Radha talks about the part in the opera *Turandot* where the slave girl, Liu, offers her life as the supreme gift to Lord Calaf, whom she loves. She asks us what the supreme gift is that we would offer. I say that life is precious. When I see how the Divine has guided and protected me, then I can show my gratitude by offering back to the Divine what I can in this life.

Swami Radha looks intensely at me and says, "But you have always done what you wanted, so where is the sacrifice?"

I immediately feel unsure of myself and say, "I didn't think the gift had to involve a sacrifice, but perhaps the supreme gift does."

"Would you have walked out of your marriage for the spiritual life?" By this time I am not thinking clearly and I don't remember what I answer. Later I realize that I had walked out of my marriage. I found my own place and turned my attention to my spiritual direction. But that was not a sacrifice because the marriage was not working. Perhaps she was thinking about how long it took me to put into action what my higher self had been telling me. Or did she mean the question in terms of an ideal marriage? Would I have left that for the spiritual life? I don't know.

I think about the preciousness of life. I could do nothing here on Earth if I had not been given life. Can I ever give back enough to make up for the gift of life? If I am not called upon to sacrifice my life, then perhaps that is not my destiny. I don't think I have the stamina and the courage to go through experiences such as the Tibetans have endured under the Chinese invasion. Perhaps I am not strong enough this time around to do that. Or perhaps I had such experiences in another life.

Development is step by step. I probably have much to learn and experience. But I do know that I move slowly when making changes.

November 24, 1995

This morning Swami Radha takes a little walk around the apartment checking on things. She stops to look carefully at one of the images a devotee gave her at the mantra pronouncement. Then we move out to the porch to sit and talk.

"What do you think is your most difficult area of surrender?" she asks me, and I find it hard to think on the spur of the moment. What comes to mind is being challenged recently on rearranging the cupboards in the kitchen without asking anyone else before doing it.

I tell her, "The kitchen is hard because it brings up old patterns of control and wanting to do things my way."

"So use that. If you take that one thing and really work with it, many of the other things will drop away and you will get there fast. Another way is to use the surrender practice, but you have to start with the most difficult person.

"Back in the early days of the Ashram I completely surrendered to one of the young men for a certain period of time just to test my ability to surrender. The practice was to surrender to whatever he suggested. I put him in the Light every day for a week before starting. This is an important preparation, as he was to be an instrument of the Divine. It meant trusting in the Divine completely and learning to surrender with faith. Because I couldn't go against his wishes or plans, the Ashram lost $2000. That was a lot in those days, but it was just money and I knew we could always get more. But remember that you don't go against your conscience in surrendering to the other person, and you don't tell the person what you are doing."

I tried this practice with a person I was having difficulty with a number of years ago, and I discovered how much I had been using resistance and self-will in my interactions. I also felt more understanding and compassion as our relationship softened somehow.

She continues, "When you started sending me your spiritual diary sheets back in the '80s, I saw your potential. You were the only one who did that."

I am surprised at this and wonder if I have followed through on that potential.

"But you overdo things. You need to be more aware. You are too willing to move in too fast to do things yourself, such as picking me up out of my chair instead of letting me at least try to do it myself."

Oh, gosh, I think I watch for her cues. If she reaches her hands toward me, she wants to get up by herself, so I offer my wrists as support if she wants to hold them. If she lifts her arms out to the side, she wants me to pick her up, as I need space to support her below her arms. But maybe I am not as aware as I think. It must be that control issue.

"Yesterday you should have stepped aside and let others have a chance to help me." I am silent, but my mind recalls that Yasoda seemed to be tending to her needs and when she left to get drinks for people she asked someone to take her place by Swami Radha. I moved over there instead of waiting to let someone else do it. I thought I was helping, but it was selfish.

"When people come over to visit, let them help out with me. Let them have a chance. You have plenty of time." She is probably referring to someone doing things like getting her a drink of milk or juice. I will remember this and perhaps be in the kitchen to show the person where things are.

I tell her, "I certainly don't want to come on too strong with you or do anything to hurt you."

"I know that, but you must develop more awareness. You have the intellectual capacity to understand the texts, but you need to apply them more. Just reading them isn't enough. You should stop reading and doing so many things to distract your mind. You need to concentrate and focus your mind; do practices; don't be so scattered, so distracted. You have a busy mind. This is why nothing can get through from the past. You won't be able to hear the Divine."

I know this is true. Learning to focus my mind is one of my big issues. She is pinpointing all the things I need to work on. She talks to me in a very straight but compassionate way. I feel grateful that she cares enough to tell me these things, as a best friend would do.

November 25, 1995

While helping Swami Radha get dressed I kneel in front of her to button her blouse and I pause, taking this opportunity of being physically close to her to tell her how grateful I am for the talk we had yesterday. "I'll work on those points of awareness you mentioned. Your guidance is such a help." I *namaste* to her and she smiles at me, her eyes reflecting warmth and understanding.

Later, as I sit with her while she is sleeping, I think about the ring with the freshwater pearls and how that gave her the message about the mantra pronouncement. I recall the time she gave me a three-strand necklace of pearls, explaining that they were Biwa seed pearls, grown only in the freshwater lake of Biwa in Japan. They are oblong in shape, resembling seeds – seeds of spiritual potential. The three strands represent the physical, mental and spiritual areas of my life. I think about the significance of how they are created, layers of a white substance growing around an irritant, perhaps a grain of sand planted inside the shell.

Did Swami Radha give me the necklace as a message? I remember the experience years ago of practising the Divine Light Invocation over a period of time to transform irritations and resentments from my past, almost like covering them with Light. This all takes on a new meaning as I put the pieces together, adding the importance of my given name, Margaret, meaning pearl.

Tonight I feel more confident and clear. I watch briefly part of the Indian dance video Swami Radha is watching, but then I leave to do a *pranayama* practice. I am going to take time as often as I can to do practices that will help me focus and be more single-pointed.

November 28, 1995

There is a big celebration at the Ashram. I am in Many Mansions and Swami Radha is there, trying to get a rest. I am protecting her from people who keep coming in, wanting to see her. A man comes who is very persistent. I turn him away, asking him if he thinks about her well-being. Why is he so focused on himself? I ask him intently, "Do you do the Light for her?" There are other people around. Some have gone into her bedroom. She is lying in bed all in white, glowing.

November 30, 1995

"Durgananda! Come quickly! Swami Radha is in a lot of pain." Yasoda holds the door open as she calls me from a deep sleep. She has just come for the 6:00 a.m. shift.

I jump up and run into the next room. Arnon is sitting on the bed holding Swami Radha in an upright position. Her eyes are closed, there is no sign of pain, but her breathing is very irregular. I help support her so Arnon can adjust the pillows higher. We lay her back against them. Yasoda is phoning for an ambulance. My mind is racing. What can we do? I repeat the Light mantra silently as I try to find a pulse. Am I missing it? Is her pulse normally very weak or...? I can't finish the thought. How could she leave us so quickly? Is there anything we could have done? Not if Krishna came in his chariot to take her home to be free, released from the pain and limitations of the physical form. She was ready to go.

The paramedics arrive and rush into her room to attend to her.

"Please be careful. She is a special person," Julie says. Other people have now come from the Radha Centre and we gather in the next room to do the Divine Light Invocation, releasing her to the Light. I ask Arnon what happened. She says they had a very peaceful night, and just before this happened they had watched the Three Tenors video. The last number was the aria from *Turendot*, "Vichero" – Victory. The pain came on just as she was lying down, but she didn't want Arnon to call anyone. She turned to give Arnon a hug, and then Yasoda arrived.

Arrangements are made to take her to the hospital. A couple of people go with her in the ambulance. The rest go to the prayer room at Radha Centre to chant the mantra for her. I stay behind to get dressed and – then what? It is so quiet, completely still. The wind blew hard all night, rattling the windows and doors. But now all is still.

"*Let's have a cup of Durgananda coffee,*" she often said with a twinkle in her eye. It really isn't much different from the way other people make coffee, but she always thought mine had a bit more flavour. I stop to listen – there is nothing but silence. I am aware of her scent, feeling her presence. I move as if in a dream as I straighten things up in her room.

I go into the living room and pause to look around. Not much to do here. I check her desk. She cleaned it up yesterday, putting everything away carefully. Did she know?

Last night she asked one of the Radha Centre residents to come for a visit in the evening. They sat out on the swing talking and then watched *Turandot* together. I remembered what she had told me about letting others have their turn with her, so I stayed in the kitchen. I was reading the manuscript of Julie's book,[2] but was available if needed. I got her vitamin C ready, then gave it to the resident to give to her.

After her visitor had gone, Swami Radha wanted to talk about Julie's book. She started to come into my room, but was stopped by the towel that was under the door to keep out the draft. So she asked me

---

2   Julie McKay (Swami Lalitananda), *Glimpses of a Mystical Affair* (Spokane, WA: timeless books, 1996).

273

to come out to her desk to talk. The room was dark except for the soft light of the desk lamp that created a warm glow between us. She welcomed me into her space with a feeling of closeness and intimacy that I hadn't experienced this deeply before. Outside the wind was blowing fiercely and some of the windows were rattling, but our little space was peaceful and quiet.

We each had a glass of Dubonnet, which she sometimes brought out for special occasions. She smiled at me and asked what I thought about Julie's manuscript. I told her how poetic and absorbing I thought it was and how it transported me to another realm when I was reading it.

Then I asked her, "Did you find parts of it almost too intimate, too personal?"

She responded, "Well, I was absolutely amazed at how Julie wrote about some of my experiences. She said things that I had never told anyone. How did she know?"

She paused to sip her Dubonnet and continued. "My European upbringing didn't allow the expression of feelings. When I was about five years old I fell and skinned my knee. It was bleeding and I began to cry. My mother came in and sternly told me to stop crying; she said that I must never cry in public. So I was brought up to not show my feelings."

She went on to tell about her mother and some of the events from her past, bringing me into the reality of her early life in Germany.

"I have lived a hundred lives just in this life," she said. I recalled the photographs from the different periods of her life and how she seemed to be a woman with a hundred faces – Spanish, Japanese, Italian, German, Native American and East Indian.

Then she talked about an incident from the earliest days of the Ashram. One of the young men sneaked into the prayer room to see what she was doing so late at night. She didn't see him sitting in a dark corner as she focused on a particular practice she was doing, struggling to keep awake by walking around the room until she finished. She got very little sleep in the early years of the Ashram because of the many responsibilities she had. When she finally noticed him he told her he was amazed at her appearance, as she looked like a hundred-year-old Tibetan.

She drew me in close to her, holding my attention so that I lost all sense of time.

Standing here in front of her desk with its empty chair, I think about her life. It is hard to put all the pieces together, as there was such a wide range of experiences. She often said that if before the Second World War someone had told her she would someday be a swami she would have thought it preposterous. I keep hearing the words from her story of her experience with Divine Light on her first visit to India. She kept repeating, "The Light, Jitendra, the Light! Don't you see it?" Jitendra, a young Indian who was with her, could see nothing. "The Light, the Light, don't you see it?" Swami Radha is in the Light, but I don't see it.

She can't be gone so quickly with no warning. It was all so sudden.

I pull myself out of the memories and come back to the present, realizing there is nothing more for me to do here.

As I walk through the kitchen to the back door I notice the calendar has fallen off the wall and is lying on the floor. Such a simple thing. Time has stopped. I know now that it is over. She gave me all I need to carry on, but she will no longer be here to challenge me or give me encouragement and direction. I put the calendar on the table and walk out the door.

I drive to the hospital to join the others and am shown the little cubicle where she is lying. She looks radiant, her hair spread out on the pillow around her, her eyes closed as if sleeping peacefully. I see her face change to an American Indian elder, then a wise old Tibetan, then a mixture of both. Looking at her fragile body I think I see the covers move as if she is breathing. Is she really gone? I think of her poem about waiting for Krishna's chariot to come and take her home and I am glad for her that she is finally with the Divine, free of pain and the many responsibilities she had. Silently I express my gratitude for her life and all she has given to so many. I salute her with *namaste* and quietly leave.

> The pain of Your teasing
> Is ended
> I am at the horizon waiting
> for your chariot to take me home
> to You.
>
> – Swami Radha, "In My Heart Is a Song"

epilogue

My final contact with Swami Radha in the hospital was an ending. I knew for a fact then that my physical connection with her was over. It had all happened as my dream in February of 1980 predicted – my hand touched hers and the touch continued to the tips of our fingers as we passed by each other.

That first night after her death I slept fitfully, expecting to hear her call but heard nothing. Later there were signs that gave us all a connection to her. As her casket was driven across the border into Canada a large double rainbow appeared, the far end of it seeming to disappear into the lake right next to the Ashram. The morning of her memorial service a week later dawned cloudy and dreary, but as the temple filled with people who had come from all over to honour her, the sun's rays streamed in through all the windows. She said many times that she would always be with us in the temple. After the memorial service, her body lay on the bed in her sunroom, glowing in a white satin dress, just as in my dream on November 28th, two days before she passed into the Light. We all entered the room and walked around the bed, each of us saying goodbye in our own way.

I longed to connect with her through my dreams but it was not until January that my longing was answered. In the dream I saw images of her appearing on my inner screen. They were like video images, but they were in black and white, emerging one after another. She was smiling and talking to us about the Divine Light Invocation as if in *satsang*. I was distressed that the images were not in colour, only black and white. Did this mean that I was not really in touch with her?

The next dream I had of her was also black and white. She was standing behind me, brushing my hair back and arranging it. The mood was very light-hearted as she laughed and leaned forward, talking to me in a loving way. I have always considered my hair as a symbol of my thoughts (growing out of my head) and my self-image (having to do with appearance). So she is arranging these parts of me in a different way, showing me I can keep changing. I was happy to have this contact, but was puzzled about the lack of colour.

After this I had occasional dreams of her, but her physical form was always hazy and she was often in the background, as if observing me but not interacting. It took me years to realize that this was not to be taken in a negative sense, but was actually showing me what she had said many times. Once she is no longer in her body she will be able to contact us more easily because her earthly form will not be in the way.

This became clear to me in a recent dream I had before leading a workshop for several women. They were active, highly motivated women involved in stressful jobs or demanding relationships, and three of them had cancer. In the dream I heard instructions and knew it was Swami Radha but had no visual image of her. She was telling me about women and the use of energy. It is important for them to use their energy wisely and to conserve it for what is really important. I took this as guidance for myself, but also for the women in the workshop and I brought forward the important points she had made. I am very grateful and am putting this advice into practice as I age. I want to make this a time of grace.

But it is not through dreams alone that I connect with her. I have learned to tap into her essence and the wealth of material that she passed on to me. The threads of our lives are woven together in a tapestry that will continue to reveal its meaning for me. The past is malleable. The changes I make in my life now shed new light on those experiences and this in turn expands their meaning. Life still holds mysteries to be fathomed, making my life an adventure.

It has been ten years now since Swami Radha's death, and my spiritual evolution has continued in a deepening of my experience of surrender. It has not involved an intellectual understanding, but rather a feeling of the heart. It has grown out of my time with her and the years that she helped me to break through my limitations, but now I am taking the experience further. The seeds of Durga's strength have taken root.

Every spiritual practice she gave me is a guideline to use in living my daily life. I see also that these teachings will carry me with awareness into the transition called death, letting go of attachments, continuing to work with my connection to the Light, becoming single-pointed. There is the knowing that the Divine has been with me through the difficult times as well as the tender moments.

The thread of Dawn's story weaving through my life culminated with her *sanyas* initiation on Easter Sunday 2004. She became Swami Yasodananda, and our connection grew even closer. I initiated her, an experience that brought together the two streams of our lives like a river flowing into the Divine source. I am sure Swami Radha's essence was with us on that special day.

The confidence and sense of purpose I saw in Swami Radha at my first meeting with her in 1967 has matured in me, blossoming into a new understanding of commitment. It has also taken me to a deeper place in my inner connection to the Divine, so that I have felt the strength of Durga coming forward. The power of that inner connection has stayed with me and helps me to continue to grow.

I hear Swami Radha's words telling me over and over, "You don't know how much time you have left. Do it now."

about the author

Swami Durgananda (Margaret White) was born in Philadelphia in 1924. She was a housewife and mother of three children when she met Swami Sivananda Radha in 1967. That meeting began a life-changing journey. She went back to university to gain a fine arts degree and a master of education. She moved to Yasodhara Ashram in 1981. Eight years later she took vows of *sanyas* and became Swami Durgananda. She was the director of a Radha Centre in Victoria for four years, and continues to teach Hatha and Dream Yoga. A dedicated artist and yogini, Swami Durgananda is now the vice-president of Yasodhara Ashram.

other titles from timeless

Books by Swami Sivananda Radha:
Hatha Yoga: The Hidden Language
The Divine Light Invocation
Mantras: Words of Power
Kundalini Yoga for the West
When You First Called Me Radha: Poems
The Devi of Speech: The Goddess in Kundalini Yoga
Radha: Diary of a Woman's Search
Realities of the Dreaming Mind: The Practice of Dream Yoga

Books by other authors:
Yoga: A Gem for Women by Geeta Iyengar
Inspired Lives: The Best of Real Life Yoga from ascent magazine
    edited by Clea McDougall

Audio:
The Divine Light Invocation
Relaxation
Guided Meditation
Hari Om: Mantra for Meditation
Om Namah Sivaya: Mantra for Meditation
The Power of Mantras

resources for the teachings of swami sivananda radha

timeless books
for a free timeless catalogue or more info:
www.timeless.org
Canada toll-free: 1-800-661-8711
USA toll-free: 1-800-251-9273
contact@timeless.org

ascent magazine
To subscribe to or order back issues:
www.ascentmagazine.com
Toll-free: 1-888-825-0228
info@ascentmagazine.com

The Yasodhara Ashram
For information on courses and retreats
and to find out about classes in your city:
www.yasodhara.org
Toll-free: 1-800-661-8711
yashram@netidea.com